monsoonbooks

JOSEPH CONRAD'S EASTERN

Author and historian Ian Burnet grew up in South Gippsland in Victoria, Australia, and has spent thirty years living, working and travelling in Indonesia and wider Southeast Asia. His fascination for the diverse history and culture of the Indonesian archipelago is reflected in his numerous books set in the region.

Praise for *Joseph Conrad's Eastern Voyages*

'Fascinating ... it will lead many of us to re-read Conrad's books with new understanding.' Dr Ron Witton in *Inside Indonesia*

'Few Conrad scholars have been to many of the places that feature in his Malay fiction, and it is refreshing to read a book that contains Burnet's knowledge of Indonesia and of Singapore ... a very welcome addition to a complex area of Conrad's life and writing.' Dr Andrew Francis in *Joseph Conrad Today*, Joseph Conrad Society of America

'[Burnet] builds on Conrad's own retrospective memory and quotes liberally from the novels to connect the fictional and non-fictional worlds ... an indispensable work for anyone interested in Conrad. This is not a work of literary criticism ... [rather] an informative introduction to Conrad's life and works.' Dr John Butler, *Asian Review of Books*

'Takes us through Conrad's novels, and the various characters that inhabit them ... a great read.' Mark Heyward, author of *The Glass Islands: A year in Lombok*

OTHER BOOKS BY THE AUTHOR

Spice Islands

East Indies

Archipelago: A Journey Across Indonesia

Where Australia Collides with Asia

The Tasman Map

Joseph Conrad's
Eastern Voyages

Ian Burnet

monsoon

monsoonbooks

Published in 2024
by Monsoon Books Ltd
www.monsoonbooks.co.uk

No.1 The Lodge, Burrough Court, Burrough on the Hill,
Melton Mowbray LE14 2QS, UK.

Illustrated edition first published in 2021 by Alfred Street Press, Australia.

ISBN (paperback): 9781915310309
ISBN (ebook): 9781915310316

Copyright©Ian Burnet, 2021

Cover painting 'Macassar Quay' by JC Rappart (1883). The ship in
the painting is assumed to be the steamship *Vidar*, in which Conrad
frequently sailed from its base in Singapore to various ports in Borneo
and Sulawesi. [Photo©Nationaal Museum van Wereldculturen, Leiden.]

A Cataloguing-in-Publication data record is available from the British
Library.

MIX
Paper | Supporting
responsible forestry
FSC® C018072

Printed and bound in Great Britain by Clays Ltd, Elcograf S.p.A.
26 25 24   1 2 3

'Joseph Conrad' by George Charles Beresford (1904).
'This portrait was made the year Conrad
completed the novel *Nostromo*.'
[Photo©National Portrait Gallery, London]

Suddenly a puff of wind, a puff faint and tepid
and laden with strange odours of blossoms,
of aromatic wood, comes out of the still night –
the first sigh of the East on my face. That I can never forget.
It was impalpable and enslaving, like a charm,
like a whispered promise of mysterious delight.

Joseph Conrad, 'Youth'

Contents

Timeline

1857	The birth of Józef Teodor Konrad Korzeniowski of Polish parents in what is now Ukraine.
1861	His father Apollo Korzeniowski, poet, translator and activist is arrested for protesting against the Russian occupation of Poland/Ukraine.
1862	His early boyhood living with his parents in an internment camp for political detainees in northern Russia.
1865	The death of his mother due to the harsh conditions of internment.
1869	The death of his father due to the harsh conditions of internment.
1874	His escape from Poland to avoid Russian military conscription.
1876-1877	His 'wild years' in Marseille, gambling, debts, gun smuggling and an attempted suicide.
1878	He leaves Marseille and joins the British Merchant Marine.
1879	His voyage to Sydney on the *Duke of Sutherland*.
1880	His voyage to Sydney on the *Loch Etive*.
1880	The sinking of the Pilgrim ship *Jeddah*.
1881	His voyage to the Far East in the sailing ship *Palestine*.
1886	He becomes a British subject.

1887	His voyage to Semarang on the sailing ship *Highland Forest*.
1887-1888	His voyages to Borneo in the *Vidar*.
1888	He receives his first command as captain of the barque *Otago*.
1889	Begins to write *Almayer's Folly*.
1890	His voyage up the Congo River and into the heart of darkness.
1891-1893	Voyages around the world in the sailing ship *Torrens*.
1893	He marries Jessie George.
1894	The steamship *Adowa's* failure marks the end of Conrad's career at sea.
1895	*Almayer's Folly* is published under the name of Joseph Conrad.
1896	*An Outcast of the Islands* is published.
1899	*Heart of Darkness* is published.
1900	*Lord Jim* is published.
1912	*A Personal Record* appears in book form.
1915	*Victory* is published.
1920	*The Rescue* is published twenty-four years after its commencement.
1924	Joseph Conrad dies of a heart attack at the age of 66.

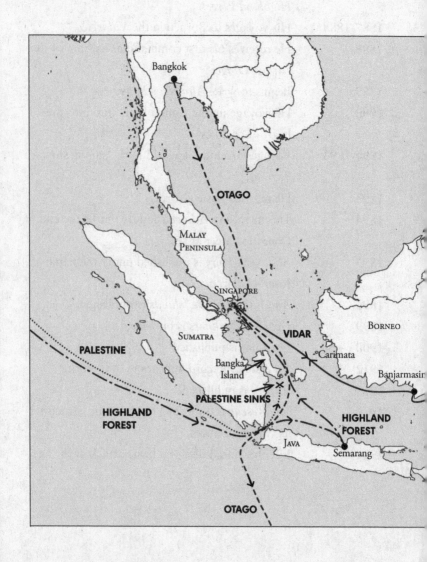

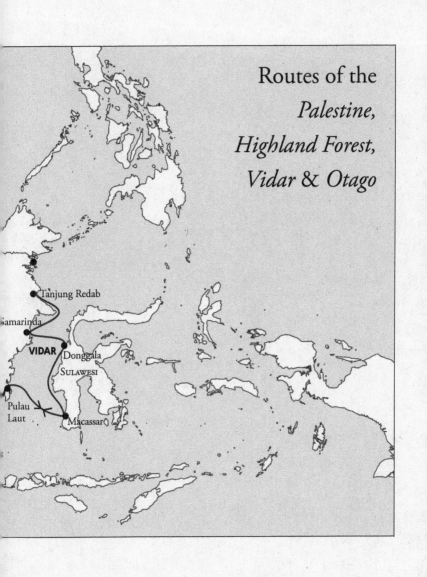

Routes of the
Palestine,
Highland Forest,
Vidar & Otago

Tanjung Redab

Samarinda

VIDAR Donggala

SULAWESI

Pulau
Laut

Macassar

Prologue

The life of Józef Teodor Konrad Korzeniowski reads like an adventure story, an adventure story written by somebody like Joseph Conrad.

During the twenty years from the time that he left Poland in October 1874 until he signed off his last vessel in January 1894, Konrad worked in ships. For fifteen of those years he served under the Red Ensign as a British merchant seaman, and Konrad describes it as 'the finest day in his life' when in 1880 and at the age of twenty-three he received his certificate as a second mate in the British Merchant Navy. Eventually Konrad would make his home in England and apply for British nationality, which was granted in 1886.

Konrad served aboard numerous ships as a crew member and then as third, second and first mate, until eventually achieving the rank of captain and command of the three-masted barque *Otago*. He lived an adventurous life at sea in the final and glorious days of sailing ships, the three-masted square-rigged ships that were the most beautiful vessels to ever sail the oceans. The seamen on these sailing ships were at one with the elements, the wind, the waves, the tides and the currents, and it required great skill to harness nature to their purpose. The sea emphasised the dependence of man upon man, and loyalty to the ship, as a condition of survival against the hostile elements of nature. It was a dangerous life and of the first seven British sailing vessels that Konrad worked, five of them were ultimately lost at sea.

Konrad's favoured destination was Asia, the bustling transit port of Singapore, the remote islands and ports of the Dutch East Indies. It was from Singapore that he made four voyages as first mate on the steamship *Vidar* to a small trading post which was forty miles up a river on the east coast of Borneo. A river and a settlement which he described as 'one of the lost, forgotten, unknown places on earth' and where he would meet the people, places and events that he describes in his first novels.

Towards the end of his sailing career, at the age of thirty-five, with no ship and no immediate prospect of a command, Konrad's days were empty. Idle in London he began to write of his experiences of the people he had met at that isolated trading post on the Berau River in eastern Borneo. The idea of writing an entire book was then outside his imagination, but the characters he had met in Borneo began to visit him in the front sitting room of his furnished apartment in a Pimlico square.

About half of everything Joseph Conrad ever wrote takes place in Southeast Asia: six novels, plus more than a dozen short stories and novellas, which are all evocative of the exotic East. Although his love was for sailing ships and the world's great oceans, his voyages on the tramp ship *Vidar* to the Java Sea, the Macassar Strait and the east coast of Borneo inspired more of Conrad's fiction than any other period in his life. His Borneo books – *Almayer's Folly*, *An Outcast of the Islands*, *Lord Jim*, *Victory* and *The Rescue* – were all based on the places he had visited, the stories he had heard, and the people he had met during his voyages in the Indonesian archipelago. It is his excellent visual memory of people, landscape, estuaries, rivers, climate, jungle foliage, commerce, local politics, religion and dress that bring his fictional world to life.

In *Almayer's Folly* Conrad introduces us to the anti-hero of his first two novels, who is based on a Dutchman born in Java known as Charles Olmeijer, the resident trader of that small outpost on the Berau River. He left a deep impression on Conrad because of the vastness of his ambitions compared to his derelict appearance and his actual situation. Conrad later wrote that 'If I had not got to know Almayer pretty well, it is almost certain there would never have been a line of mine in print'.

Almayer's Folly was published in 1895 under the anglicised name of Joseph Conrad and he then devoted himself full-time to writing. He wrote slowly, always struggling with deadlines and anxious about money. Although his work was frequently interrupted by agonising periods of writer's block and persistent illnesses, he went on to write some twenty novels as well as some of the world's greatest short fiction. His books were a critical success but he only obtained commercial success late in his career after the publication of *Chance*, one of his few novels that had a happy ending.

Conrad was important because he was an outsider who had not grown up with the popular myths of the glory of the British Empire. He became British but viewed the world from a non-British perspective and was one of the first English writers of the period to pierce the popular assumptions of superiority that had grown up around the British Empire, colonials and colonial life. The place he now occupies in letters is as the English critic Walter Allen wrote: 'Conrad's best work represents a body of achievement unequalled in English fiction this century by any writer except [Henry] James.' While Henry James wrote in a letter to Conrad: 'No one has known – for intellectual use – the things you know, and you have, as the artist of the whole matter, an authority that no one has approached.' Conrad's greatness lies in his ability to create an absolutely convincing illusion of reality and for Joseph Conrad his greatest honour was to have his novels regarded as English classics in his own lifetime and despite the fact that English was not his native language.

My interest in Conrad began when I arrived in Indonesia from the sea and as a young man around the same age as Joseph Conrad. During my years of residence and my travels throughout the Indonesian archipelago, I, like Conrad, fell in love with its people its extraordinary mixture of races, ethnic groups, religions, languages, cultures and its endlessly fascinating history.

In his writing, Conrad was able to convert actual events of his own experience into enduring fiction and he once said that everything about his life can be found in his books. Not all of Conrad's fiction is based on his real life, but the material in many of his books is mainly autobiographical and in this book I am able to use a mixture of my words, together with his, to tell this story of Joseph Conrad's eastern voyages and how he made the connection between his own life experiences and the characters and events in his first novels.

This book aims to intertwine Conrad's own reflections with

my observations and experiences in Indonesia and Singapore, offering a unique perspective that bridges past and present, fiction and reality. It is my hope that this retelling not only pays homage to Conrad's legacy but also inspires a deeper appreciation for the rich tapestry of cultures and histories that he encountered during his voyages.

1

Voyage of the *Palestine*, 1881

And this is how I see the East. I have seen its secret places
and have looked into its very soul; but now I see it always
from a small boat, a high outline of mountains, blue and afar
in the morning; like faint mist at noon; a jagged wall
of purple at sunset.

Joseph Conrad, 'Youth'

For his first voyage to the Far East, Józef Teodor Konrad
Korzeniowski found an insignificant little three-masted barque
covered in rust, dust and grime lying in a dark pool in one of the
smaller London dockyards. The *Palestine* needed a second mate,
and he appears on the ship's articles as Konrad Korzeniowski,
aged twenty-four, of Gittomir, Poland. What Konrad was looking
for was at least twelve months of certified experience as a regular
watchkeeping officer in a deep-sea vessel. The captain of the
Palestine was Elijah Beard, a gnarled seaman of the old school
who had spent his life sailing the rigours of the North Sea. A
fine old man, he had been long overlooked as this was his first

command and Konrad believed he was 'sixty if a day'. The mate was an experienced Irish seaman of fifty years who had a Roman nose and a long snow-white beard; his name was Mahon. Both were thoroughly good seamen and between these two grizzled old sailors Konrad felt like a young boy standing between two grandfathers.

In Conrad's short story 'Youth', which is essentially autobiographical, he changes the name of the *Palestine* to *Judea* and the captain from Elijah Beard to Brierly, but all other elements are almost the same. The voyage would be life-changing for Konrad because it would bring him to the Far East, to Singapore, to the Malay Archipelago and to the Dutch East Indies, places that would become the background for his first books: *Almayer's Folly, An Outcast of the Island* and *Lord Jim*.

The *Palestine* had been laid up for such a long time that she was covered in dust, soot and dirt. However, underneath all this grime she was a well-built British wooden sailing vessel, a barque of symmetrical rig and graceful form. As Conrad first describes her in 'Youth':

> To me it was like coming out of a palace into a ruined
> cottage. She was about 400 tons, had a primitive windlass,
> wooden latches to the doors, not a bit of brass about her,
> and a big square stern. There was on it, below her name
> in big letters, a lot of scroll work, with the gilt off, and
> some sort of a coat of arms, with the motto 'Do or Die'
> underneath. I remember it took my fancy immensely.
> There was a touch of romance in it, something that made

me love the old thing – something that appealed to my youth!

The *Palestine* departed London on 21 September 1881, reaching Newcastle and the River Tyne where it remained for five weeks loading its cargo of coal. The vessel then left Newcastle in November with six hundred tons of coal to deliver across the Indian Ocean and halfway around the world to Bangkok in Thailand. This was Konrad's first voyage as a ship's officer and his first voyage to what he described as the mysterious East. At only twenty-four years of age his voyage on the *Palestine* was going to be a great adventure:

> O Youth! The strength of it, the faith of it, the imagination
> of it! To me she was not an old rattle-trap carting about
> the world a lot of coal for a freight – to me she was the
> endeavour, the test, the trial of life. I think of her with
> pleasure, with affection, with regret – as you would think
> of someone dead you have loved. I shall never forget her.

A new technical innovation had completely revolutionised sea freight. Built in Britain in 1839, the oak-hulled SS *Archimedes* was the world's first screw propeller-driven steamship designed for open-water voyages. Screw propulsion had considerable influence on ship development and its positive effect on commercial vessels resulted in its adoption by the Royal Navy. Ten years later the revolutionary SS *Great Britain*, built by Brunel, became the first iron-hulled *and* screw-driven ship, the first ship to combine these two innovations and the first ship of its type to cross the Atlantic. In the beginning, these first ocean-going steamships also kept their sails because they could not carry enough coal or water for long-distance voyages and their engines were not always reliable. However, the greater size and reliability of steamships allowed them to load much more freight than sailing ships and, importantly, the insurance premiums for their cargo were much less.

The opening of the Suez Canal in 1869 cut three thousand eight hundred miles off the journey from London to China and gave the steamships a critical advantage over sailing vessels on the busy Europe to Asia route. The canal was not a practical option for sailing vessels, as using a tug to haul them through was expensive. Steamships immediately made use of this new waterway and found themselves in high demand in China for the start of the 1870 tea season. So successful was steamship trade using the Suez Canal that forty-five new steamships were built in the Clyde shipyards in 1871 for the Eastern trade.

Coal was needed to fuel the iron steamships that were now traversing the world's oceans and coal bunkers were positioned at ports around the world. To the regret of many, including a whole breed of ocean-going sailors, graceful sailing ships were converted into grimy coal colliers. However, it was much more difficult for the steamship to take over the long-haul trades to Australia, New Zealand, Chile and California which entailed rounding the Cape of Good Hope or Cape Horn and it was on these routes that sailing ships lasted well into the twentieth century.

By 1883 the total tonnage of British steamships exceeded that of sail for the first time. The total tonnage had risen as the size of the iron steamships increased but the total number of vessels declined and it was estimated that two hundred and sixty shipmasters lost employment every year. This was not a good time to be employed as a merchant seaman but despite all these difficulties Konrad refused to go into steam as he loved the fine lines and character of the great sailing ships of the day. Competition with steam meant that sailing ships increasingly carried too much canvas, with too few men to safely work these ships. It was a dangerous life and Conrad wrote:

> Like a beautiful and unscrupulous woman, the sea of the past was glorious in its smile, irresistible in its anger, capricious, enticing, illogical, irresponsible, a thing of love, a thing of fear. It cast a spell, it gave joy, it lulled gently into boundless faith, then with quick and causeless anger it killed. But its cruelty was redeemed by the charm of its inscrutable mystery, by the immensity of its promise, by the supreme witchery of its possible favour. Strong men with childlike hearts were faithful to it, were content to live by its grace – to die by its will.

The *Palestine* departed Newcastle in beautiful sunny winter weather which lasted all the way down the North Sea, the English Channel and three hundred miles out into the Atlantic Ocean before the wind came around to the southwest and as described by Conrad:

In the stormy space surrounding us there was as much flying spray as air. Day after day and night after night there was nothing round the ship but the howl of the wind, the tumult of the sea, the noise of water pouring over her deck. There was no rest for her and no rest for us. She tossed, she pitched, she stood on her head, she sat on her tail, she rolled, she groaned, and we had to hold on while on deck and cling to our bunks when below, in a constant effort of body and worry of mind.

The *Palestine* started taking on water, forcing the crew to man the pumps in four-hour shifts. According to Conrad they pumped all night, all day, all week. They pumped for dear life, watch after watch and for their exhausted bodies it seemed like an eternity:

And we pumped. And there was no break in the weather. The sea was white like a sheet of foam. Like a cauldron of boiling milk: there was not a break in the clouds, no – not the size of a man's hand, no – not for so much as ten seconds. There was for us no stay, there were for us no stars, no sun, no universe – nothing but angry clouds and an infuriated sea. We pumped watch and watch for dear life ... we had forgotten how it felt to be dry.

Despite the conditions, this was a great test for Konrad – as second mate he had to supervise his crew, not only 'to keep his chaps up to the mark' as he describes it, but to work alongside them and to 'keep himself up to the mark'. It was a life-confirming

experience and like the words written on the ship's stern –
'*Palestine*, London. Do or Die' – Konrad and his vessel braved
the worst of the elements and survived. If he did not know this
already, Konrad soon learned that life on a ship was a unique life
and demanded the total loyalty and discipline of its crew. Not
from any terms of service or compulsion by its officers, but as a
means of one's own survival.

Once the storm abated the *Palestine* was forced to return to
Falmouth for repairs. Strained beyond endurance she had spat
out all the oakum that sealed her lower seams. Most of the crew
considered she was unsafe, refused duty, and deserted the ship
in Falmouth. The initial and hasty repairs did not fix the real
problems and after another failed voyage her owners decided
that the *Palestine* needed a complete refit. Because of numerous
delays the repairs took eight months; she was completely re-
calked, given a copper bottom and, according to Konrad, made
as tight as a bottle. Konrad remained with the ship throughout
her time in port in order to gain the time in service required for
his first mate's examination. Falmouth was good to Konrad.
He had more leisure time and was able to indulge his favourite
activity, which was reading and mastering the English language.
He was able to go up to London to collect some books and recalls
reading the dramatic works of William Shakespeare to the noisy
accompaniment of caulkers' mallets driving oakum into the dry
seams of the *Palestine*. However, the mysterious East still awaited,
and he wrote:

And for me there was also my youth to make me patient.

There was all the East before me, and all life, and the thought that I had been tried in that ship and had come out pretty well. And I thought of men of old who, centuries ago, went that road in ships that sailed no better, to the land of palms, and spices, and yellow sands, and of brown nations ruled by kings more cruel than Nero the Roman and more splendid than Solomon the Jew.

Already a year after its initial departure from London, the *Palestine* finally departed Falmouth for Bangkok with its cargo of coal on 17 September 1882. The voyage down the Atlantic Ocean was now literally smooth sailing. She rounded the Cape of Good Hope without stopping at Cape Town and entered the Indian Ocean whence she sailed due south to catch the Roaring Forties. However, the winds were light and weeks slipped by as the *Palestine* lumbered eastward towards that point in the Indian Ocean where their calculation of longitude told them they were due south of the Sunda Strait, between the islands of Sumatra and Java, and it was time to turn north:

The old barque lumbered on, heavy with her age and the burden of her cargo, while I lived the life of youth in ignorance and hope. She lumbered on through an interminable procession of days; and the fresh gilding flashed back at the setting sun, seemed to cry out over the darkening sea the words painted on her stern, '*Judea*, London. Do or Die'.

Coal is a dangerous cargo, especially when it has been too long aboard and too often wet. So serious was the risk of fire in coal cargoes that the subject had been considered by a Royal Commission in 1875 because of the number of coal-laden ships lost due to self-combustion of their cargo. It was reported that fifty-seven coal-laden ships were known to have been lost because of their burning cargo and an appalling total of three hundred and twenty-eight crew were reported as missing at sea. The Royal Commission reported that the principal factors identified were the quality of the coal as lower quality coals were more prone to self-heating, smaller coal lump size was also more prone to self-heating, and the wetness of the coal was a factor. It went on to say that the self-heating was caused by oxidation of the coal, with the combustion going through several stages prior to flaming ignition.

Somewhere in the Indian Ocean, Conrad described in his short story 'Youth' how when he unlocked the forepeak there was a heavy, sooty smell of paraffin – the coal had started to combust! The next day the vessel began to smoke in earnest. The coal had broken into smaller lumps in the transfer to a storage hulk in Falmouth then it had become wet in rain on the journey back from the hulk. This was another case of spontaneous combustion, although there was no sign of fire as without sufficient oxygen the coal only smouldered down below.

Captain Beard called the crew to his cabin. He had a chart spread out on the table and explained that the coast of Western Australia was near but since it was the cyclone season, they would proceed to Java Head and would try to stifle the combustion by want of air. They battened down all the hatches and still she smoked. The smoke kept seeping through the bulkheads and the covers and made its way into every part of the ship. Clearly, if smoke was escaping out then air was getting in. The only other solution was water and Conrad describes how they poured half of the Indian Ocean into the main hatch:

> Steam ascended mingling with the smoke. We poured salt water as into a barrel without a bottom. It was our fate to pump in that ship, to pump out of her, to pump into her; and after keeping water out of her to save ourselves from being drowned, we now frantically poured water into her to save ourselves from being burnt.

After flooding the bottom of the ship with water the smoke diminished and in two days there was no smoke at all. There were broad grins all around. The crew cleaned themselves up for the first time in a fortnight and all partook of a special dinner. They spoke of spontaneous combustion with contempt and celebrated their success in extinguishing the smouldering cargo. Then, as described by Conrad:

> Next day it was my watch on deck from eight to twelve. At breakfast the captain observed, 'It's wonderful how that smell hangs about the cabin.' About ten, the mate being on the poop, I stepped down on the main-deck for a moment. The carpenter's bench stood abaft the mainmast: I leaned against it sucking at my pipe, and the carpenter, a young chap, came to talk to me. He remarked, 'I think

we have done very well, haven't we?' and then I perceived with annoyance the fool was trying to tilt the bench. I said curtly, 'Don't, Chips,' and immediately became aware of a queer sensation, of an absurd delusion, – I seemed somehow to be in the air. I heard all round me like a pent-up breath released – as if a thousand giants simultaneously had said Phoo! – and felt a dull concussion which made my ribs ache suddenly. No doubt about it – I was in the air, and my body was describing a short parabola. But short as it was, I had the time to think several thoughts in, as far as I can remember, the following order: 'This can't be the carpenter – What is it? – Some accident – Submarine volcano? – Coals, gas! – By Jove! We are being blown up –Everybody's dead – I am falling into the after-hatch – I see fire in it.'

The deck was a wilderness of smashed timber, lying crosswise like trees in a forest after a hurricane; an immense curtain of soiled rags waved gently in the air which was the mainsail blown to strips. The deck was a tangle of planks on edge, of planks on end, of splinters, of ruined woodwork and the masts rose from the chaos like towering trees above a matted undergrowth:

The first person I saw was Mahon, with eyes like saucers, his mouth open, and the long white hair standing straight on end round his head like a silver halo. He was just about to go down when the sight of the main deck stirring, heaving up, and changing into splinters before

31

his eyes, petrified him on the top step. I stared at him in unbelief, and he stared at me in a queer kind of shocked curiosity. I did not know that I had no hair, no eyebrows, no eyelashes and that my young moustache was burnt off, that my face was black, one cheek laid open, my nose cut, and my chin bleeding.

A passing steamer offered to tow the *Palestine* to Batavia (Jakarta) but the speed of their vessel only fanned the flames. She was now completely on fire and there was nothing that could save her or the crew. The crew abandoned the ship for the three tenders – the long boat, the second boat and a smaller boat – and these three boats drifted clear of the ship. Konrad was assigned to the smaller fourteen-foot boat and so received his first command. He had been ordered to keep close to the long boat in case of bad weather:

And do you know what I thought? I thought I would part company as soon as I could. I wanted to have my first command all to myself. I wasn't going to sail in a squadron if there were a chance for independent cruising. I would make land by myself. I would beat the other boats. Youth! All youth! The silly, charming, beautiful youth.

The captain and her crew had an obligation to its owners and insurers to see the last of their ship. The three boats, rafted up, drifted together the whole night, heaving and settling on the swell until they finally saw the last gasp of the *Palestine*:

> A magnificent death had come like a grace, like a gift, like
> a reward to that old ship at the end of her laborious days.
> The surrender of her weary ghost to the keeping of stars
> and sea was stirring like the sight of a glorious triumph.
> The masts fell just before daybreak, and for a moment
> there was a burst and turmoil of sparks that seemed to
> fill with flying fire the night patient and watchful, the vast
> night lying silent upon the sea. At daylight she was only
> a charred shell, floating still under a cloud of smoke and
> bearing a glowing mass of coal within.

As the lifeboats pulled across her stern, a slim dart of fire
shot out viciously and suddenly down she went, bow first, in a
great hiss of steam. The unconsumed stern was the last to sink
but the paint was gone – cracked and peeled off – and there were
no letters, no words, no final threat to 'Do or Die' from the good
ship *Palestine*.

Having been rafted up together, the three boats of survivors
were then cast off from each other. Konrad sat steering his first
command with nothing but water and sky around him. He had
two men with him, a bag of biscuits, a few tins of meat and some
water. Two men worked the oars while he whose turn it was to
rest held the steering oar head on into a breaking sea. There were
days and nights of calm when the boat seemed to stand still as if
bewitched within the circle of the sea horizon. He remembered
the heat, the deluge of rain squalls that filled their tiny water cask

and then sixteen hours on end with a mouth as dry as cinder. In the afternoon, Konrad sighted the upper sails of a ship far away but said nothing, and his men did not notice. He was afraid she might be homeward bound and he had no wish to turn back from his first vision of the East:

> And this is how I see the East. I have seen its secret places and have looked into its very soul; but now I see it always from a small boat, a high outline of mountains, blue and afar in the morning; like faint mist at noon; a jagged wall of purple at sunset. I have the feel of the oar in my hand, the vision of a scorching blue sea in my eyes. And I see a bay, a wide bay, smooth as glass and polished like ice, shimmering in the dark. A red light burns far off upon the gloom of the land, and the night is soft and warm. We drag at the oars with aching arms, and suddenly a puff of wind, a puff faint and tepid and laden with strange odours of blossoms, of aromatic wood, comes out of the still night – the first sigh of the East on my face. That I can never forget. It was impalpable and enslaving, like a charm, like a whispered promise of mysterious delight.

Steering for the red light, they entered the bay, tied up against the end of a jutting wharf and collapsed with exhaustion. In due time the rest of the crew from the *Palestine* reached the bay in the other two boats. For Konrad this was the achievement of his dreams: he had become the captain of his first vessel, the unnamed fourteen-foot boat that took him and his small crew to safety, and he had his first encounter with the mysterious East:

> For me all the East is contained in that vision of my
> youth. It is all in that moment when I opened my young
> eyes on it. I came upon it from a tussle with the sea – and
> I was young – and I saw it looking at me. And this is all
> that is left of it! Only a moment; a moment of strength, of
> romance, of glamour – of youth!

The officers and crew were taken to Singapore on the British steamship *Sissie* where they joined the forest of masts anchored in the harbour and were greeted by numerous sampans ready to take them ashore. About them lay hundreds of Chinese tongkangs and Malay prows unloading goods from the trading vessels lined up in what they called the 'Roads of Singapore'. This was Konrad's first view of Singapore and before him lay Johnstone Pier, the Harbour Master's Office, the entrance to the Singapore River and the warehouses storing goods that were often in trans-shipment to Hong Kong, the Malay Peninsula and the Indonesian archipelago. At the heart of the vista was Government Hill, with its verdant lawns and large bungalow. Below that lay the European town, the mansions of the merchant princes, St Andrews Cathedral and Sailors' Home. If he had looked closely, Konrad could also have seen the European hospital overlooking the harbour.

Records show that Konrad was discharged on 3 April 1883 and remained in Singapore for the whole of April. More than likely, he would have stayed in Sailors' Home and explored the port area including the Harbour Office, the offices of the various shipping agents and the various cafés and bars where seamen congregated to swap stories and compare voyages.

Singapore was the centre of all the archipelago trade – from Borneo, the Straits Settlements of Penang and Malacca on the Malay Peninsula, from Sumatra, Java and the thousands of islands in the Dutch East Indies. The East with its whispered promise of mysterious delight would remain part of Joseph Conrad's life, both through his voyages to eastern ports and in his first books.

'Youth' is a great adventure story and finishes with its author's introduction to the Far East, but who was Józef Teodor Konrad Korzeniowski and what had brought him to this point in his life?

2

Early Life

Józef Teodor Konrad Korzeniowski was born on 3 December 1857 in Berdychiv, a city in one of the Ukrainian provinces of Poland under Russian Tsarist rule. His parents, Apollo Korzeniowski and Ewelina Bobrowska, were of the Polish gentry and his father Apollo was a writer, translator and by force of circumstance, a political activist.

Poland had been dismembered by its larger neighbours, Russia, Prussia and Austria, so that by the time Konrad was born it had ceased to officially exist. Although the vast majority of the surrounding area's inhabitants were Ukrainians, almost all the countryside was owned by the Polish nobility, to which Konrad's family belonged as bearers of the Nalecz coat of arms. Despite the demise of their national independence, Polish history, language, literature and culture remained, and the Poles retained that fierce patriotism for which they are still distinguished.

Konrad's father Apollo belonged to the 'Red' political faction, whose goal was to re-establish the pre-partition boundaries of Poland, but also advocated land reform and the abolition of serfdom. Apollo was consumed by two passions: his love of literature and a fierce desire to liberate his country from Russian domination. His fervent wish was that his son would see the restoration of the 'stolen lands' within his lifetime. In pursuit of his literary career, he moved to Warsaw in 1861 where he became involved in publishing a political pamphlet, formed the underground City Committee and played a prominent role in the revolutionary activities of the period. For these activities, Apollo and his wife, Ewe, were arrested, convicted of seditious activities and sentenced to exile in an internment camp at Volgoda in northern Russia.

Apollo was accompanied in exile by his wife and the four-year-old Konrad, and life in the camp meant that the family's health suffered much during their time there. Inevitably, little Konrad was neglected. In a letter to relatives, Apollo wrote of their appalling conditions:

> Volgoda is a great marsh, cut up with parallel and intersecting lines of wooden foot-bridges, all rotting and shaky under one's feet. The climate consists of two seasons a year: a white winter and a green winter. The white winter lasts nine and a half months and the green one two and a half. We are now at the onset of the green winter: it has already been raining ceaselessly for twenty-one days. The population is a nightmare of disease-ridden corpses.

Konrad's father spent his time in exile translating literary giants such as Victor Hugo, Charles Dickens and Shakespeare into Polish. As a result of their miserable conditions both his parents contracted tuberculosis and were moved further south to Chernikhov. In 1865, when Konrad was only seven, his mother, Ewe, died. His father buried himself in grief and wrote in despair:

> Should I describe this place I would say that on one side it is bounded by locked doors behind which the being dearest to me breathed her last, without my being able to wipe even the death sweat from her brow, while on the other ... I see what Dante did not describe.

For the next three years, Konrad was to live a strange, isolated life, alone with his father in their exile. His father translated the works of James Fenimor Cooper including *The Deerslayer* and *The Prairie*, as well as the plays of Shakespeare such as *Much Ado About Nothing*, *As You Like It*, *The Two Gentlemen of Verona*, *A Comedy Errors* and *Othello*. His father wrote that young Konrad would read some of these when he was only eight or nine years old. Konrad's devotion to literature, interest in revolutionary politics, attitudes about Russia, his adventurous spirit and sceptical view of the world probably all came from that period. His first acquaintance with Charles Dickens, another writer his father admired, began at an early age and Conrad wrote that:

> My first introduction to English imaginative literature was "Nicholas Nickleby." It is extraordinary how well Mrs. Nickleby could chatter disconnectedly in Polish and the sinister Ralph rage in that language. As to the Crummles family and the family of the learned Squeers it

seemed as natural to them as their native speech. It was, I have no doubt, an excellent translation.

By 1867 his father was seriously ill and was given permission to return from exile to Krakow. Two weeks before his death in 1869, Konrad watched his father burning some of his manuscripts and letters, an act which he describes as not so much that of a man desperately ill but that of a vanquished man who was mortally weary. Konrad must have been deeply affected by the heroic nature of his parents' protest, yet he had seen their idealism result only in the miseries of exile and their deaths. His father is still considered a national hero in Poland and was given a hero's burial. The funeral took the form of a patriotic tribute, with the eleven-year-old Konrad walking at the head of a great procession, which he later described:

> I could see again the small boy of that day following a hearse; a space kept clear in which I walked alone, conscious of an enormous following, the clumsy swaying of the tall black machine, the chanting of the surplice clergy ... the rows of bared heads on the pavements with fixed, serious eyes. Half the population had turned out on that fine May afternoon.

The orphaned Konrad was cared for by his grandmother and in particular by his maternal uncle Tadeusz Bobrowski who became a second father to him and would guide his future for many more years. It was clear that his uncle hoped to steer the young Konrad in the footsteps of his own pragmatic self rather than his romantic father when he wrote:

> It has pleased God to strike you with the greatest misfortune that can assail a child – the loss of his parents. But in his goodness God has so graciously allowed your very good grandmother and myself to look after you, your health, your studies and your future destiny. Without a thorough education you will be worth nothing in this world, so master the beginnings of every subject with work and determination, study not that which is easy and attractive, but that which is useful.

It was in Krakow that Konrad first started his formal schooling. Because of his upbringing, he was intellectually well developed but he hated the rigours of school, which tired and bored him. He would say that he had a great deal of talent and would become a great writer. This coupled with a sarcastic smile on his face and frequent critical remarks on everything and everybody, provoked surprise in his teachers and ridicule from the other students.

When Konrad turned seventeen he was liable for conscription into the Russian army. As a result of his parents' revolutionary activities and his own internment, he could be viewed as an enemy of the state and his conscription could be as long as twenty years. The young Konrad had expressed a wish to go to sea, an idea unheard of in rural Poland but perhaps derived from his youthful reading of adventure stories and his father's translation of *Toilers of the Sea* by Victor Hugo. Konrad had to leave Poland and, despite his reservations, his uncle sent the sixteen-year-old to Marseilles, France, for a planned career at sea. For the young Konrad, leaving his homeland for an uncertain future would have been difficult, but everything he knew of his homeland was filled with memories of tragedy and loss. Leaving was imperative although his decision to not follow in his father's footsteps and to choose exile over resistance was a source of lifelong guilt.

Konrad arrived in France as an undocumented foreign national but thanks to his uncle he had a personal introduction to a Monsieur Delestang, a shipowner in Marseille. Konrad was seeking adventure and his first day at sea, with the wind in his hair and the salt spray on his face, would have been a memorable one, and he wrote of his first sailing experience in his autobiography *A Personal Record*:

> The very first whole day I ever spent on salt water was by invitation, in a big half decked pilot-boat, cruising under close reefs on the look-out, in mist, blowing weather, for the sails of ships and the smoke of steamers ... And many a day and night too did I spend cruising with these rough, kindly men ... Their sea-tanned faces, whiskered or shaved, lean or full, with the intent wrinkled sea-eyes of the pilot breed, and here and there a thin gold loop at the lobe of a hairy ear, bent over my sea infancy.

Young, free of Russian internment and his uncle's influence, his time in Marseille was chaotic. He spent money he didn't have, resorted to gambling to try and cover his losses and apparently took part in the illegal shipment of arms from France into Spain in support of the Carlists and the pretender to the Spanish throne, Don Carlos V. He also seems to have fallen in love with a girl who was also implicated in the Carlist plot. Conrad used this period as material for his book *The Arrow of Gold* and wrote of his arms smuggling activities:

> I must say that for the next three months I threw myself into my unlawful trade with a sort of desperation, dogged and hopeless, like a fairly decent fellow who takes deliberately to drink. The business was getting dangerous. The bands in the South were not very well organised, worked with no very definite plan, and now were beginning to be pretty closely hunted. The arrangements for the transport of supplies were going to pieces; our friends ashore were getting scared; and it was no joke to find after a day of skilful dodging that there was no one at the landing place and have to go out again with our compromising cargo.

Tadeusz Bobrowski had agreed to send his nephew an allowance of one thousand francs a year. Because of his propensity to spend money he did not have and the piling up of debt, there is evidence that early in 1878 Konrad attempted suicide. However, his reliable Uncle Tadeusz seemed always willing to bail him out when necessary, as detailed in this letter:

> I learned that you have drawn from the bank in one sum your allowance for the eight months from January until

October, and having lent it (or possibly squandered it) you are in need. Subsequently in May you wrote to me apologising but not offering any clear explanation. At last on 21 May you sent a telegram requesting an order for 700 francs which was paid to you on 2 July: again in answer to another telegraphic request I ordered 400 francs to be paid out to you, and on departing from Marseilles you wrote asking me to pay 165 francs to a friend of yours - Mr, Bonnard, who had lent you this sum and I did.

Konrad spent nearly four years in France and on French ships as a passenger and as an apprentice, but he needed a valid passport to progress through the French maritime service. Because of the risk of conscription, he had left Russia without a passport and the Russian consular officials in France now refused to issue him one unless he returned to Russia, a risk he was not prepared to take. The British merchant service had considerable advantages for someone like Konrad who was not properly documented. Because of the rapid development of steamships, the British merchant service needed seamen in large and growing numbers. As long as these could be found conscious and preferably sober, nobody really cared where they came from and what documents they had or didn't have.

His uncle had encouraged Konrad to seek naturalisation elsewhere, so from Marseille he joined the British ship *Mavis*, a coal freighter bound first for Constantinople and then returning with a cargo of linseed consigned to Lowestoft in England. On

18 June 1878, Konrad Korzeniowski set foot upon English soil for the first time and soon found another ship, the *Skimmer of the Seas*, a coaster with which he made six trips from Lowestoft to Newcastle, carrying four hundred tons of coal back from there each time. In later life, he would look back on his North Sea voyages and the comradeship he received from its seamen with great affection. In his *Notes on Life and Letters*, he wrote:

> The North Sea was my finishing class of seamanship before I launched myself into the wider oceans ... My teachers had been the sailors of the Norfolk shore: coast men, with steady eyes, mighty limbs, and gentle voice; men of very few words, which at least were never bare of meaning. Honest, strong, steady men, sobered by domestic ties.

Now ready to sail on the world's oceans, Konrad moved to London in October 1878. He made the railway journey from Lowestoft to London with only the address of a shipping agent and a few pounds in his pocket. He emerged from Liverpool Street station into a London that he knew only from his reading of Charles Dickens, feeling like an explorer about to penetrate a vast wilderness. As he describes in his *Notes on Life and Letters*:

> The address of an obscure shipping agent, was in my pocket. And I needed not to take it out. That address was as if graven deep in my brain. I muttered its words to myself as I walked on, navigating the sea of London by the chart concealed in the palm

of my hand; for I had vowed to myself not to inquire the way from anyone.

The address was not easy to find in the maze of the city and what he found was a tiny office, so dark that a gas jet was burning although it was one o'clock in the afternoon. Everything he knew about London came from his youthful reading of Charles Dickens and he describes finding his shipping agent, a man with a long white beard and curly white hair perched in a Dickensian office and eating a mutton chop bought from some Dickensian eating-house around the corner. However, the shipping agent was able to find him a berth on the *Duke of Sutherland,* a wool clipper bound for Sydney, Australia. With his limited British sailing experience and limited English language, Konrad could not have signed on as an able seaman and his position was as an apprentice at nominal pay but assigned to the half-deck which was reserved for lads of better family and education than the normal able seamen.

The clipper was a merchant sailing ship designed for speed, unusually narrow for its length with three masts and a square rig. The amount of canvas stretched above the ship and set tier upon tier was impressive as there were upper topsails, topgallants, royals, staysails, spanker sails and jibs. All the young men were required to climb the rigging and set the sails up or down, depending on the wind conditions, while balancing one hundred feet above a pitching ship on a small rope footline. Clearly, it was not a job for the weak or the faint-hearted. The boom years of the clipper ship era began in 1843 as a result of a growing demand for a more rapid delivery of tea from China and continued under the stimulating influence of the discovery of gold in California and Australia in 1848 and 1851. The next generation of clipper ships were iron-hulled and these continued in the Australian wool and grain trade into the early 1900s.

As the *Duke of Sutherland* approached the mid-Atlantic, the crew began the heavy task of changing from their storm sails to fair-weather sails. There were thirty-one fore-and-aft and square storm sails to come down, to be replaced by the same number of old, patched fair-weather sails. This was repeated when the *Duke of Sutherland* reached the southern latitudes, the storm sails went up again and the ship began flying at fourteen knots with all its canvas at full stretch. It usually took one hundred and nine days for the *Duke of Sutherland* to sail from London to Sydney, but heavy gales and unfavourable trade winds slowed their progress and Konrad suffered from 'imperfect oilskins which let water in at every seam'. So it was a relief to all on board when they finally reached Sydney on 31 January 1879 and docked at Circular Quay.

After unloading, the ship docked on the west side of the quay which provided easy access to the crowded streets, markets, pubs and brothels in the area known as 'The Rocks'. With no money, nowhere to go and no friends, Konrad chose to remain on board the ship, earning his meals and accommodation in return for sitting at the gangplank all night as a night watchman. The tinkle of pianos and the chorus of songs from the many pubs floated through the clear night air. From his position dockside, he could see the seamier side of the port, including drunken brawls, police patrols and on at least one occasion he received a black eye in the process of stopping a thief who, while hotly pursued, had tried to seek refuge on board, and Conrad wrote:

> I do not regret the experience. The night humours of the
> town descended from the street to the waterside in the
> still watches of the night: larrikins rushing down in bands
> to settle some quarrel by a stand-up fight, away from the
> police, in an indistinct ring half hidden by piles of cargo,
> with the sound of blows, a groan now and then.

Most sailors in their early twenties would have found such
time on ship irksome and would have preferred to explore the
town, but Konrad had so much to look at with the comings and
goings of the docks that he did not mind the confinement. He
described Sydney Harbour as 'one of the finest, most beautiful,
vast, and safe bays the sun ever shone upon' and a plaque with
this description has been placed on the same position on the
dockside where he spent his time at Circular Quay.

The Duke of Sutherland had a prolonged stay of five months
in Sydney before returning around Cape Horn with bales of wool,
bags of wheat and other assorted cargo, allowing the young
Konrad to complete his first circumnavigation of the world. We
are fortunate that a young Sydney man named Henry Horning,
embarking on his first voyage to England, describes the man who
occupied the bunk above him and indicates that he was more
than an ordinary seaman. 'He was a Pole of dark complexion and
black hair ... In his watches below, he spent all his time reading
and writing English: he spoke with a foreign accent. I can well
remember his favourite habit of sitting in his bunk with his legs

dangling over the side with either a book or writing material on his lap.' Rounding Cape Horn in winter would never be easy and Conrad writes how storms had driven them far south, much further south than they had meant to go. He describes standing on the bridge when his shoulder was gripped with such force that he cried with pain:

Look, sir! Look!

At first I saw nothing. The sea was one empty wilderness of black and white hills. Suddenly, half concealed in the tumult of foaming rollers I made out awash, something enormous, rising and falling – something spread out like a burst of foam, but with a more bluish, more solid look.

It was a piece of an ice-flow, melted down to a fragment, but still big enough to sink a ship, and floating lower than any raft, right in our way... Had it been an hour later, nothing could have saved the ship, for no eye could have made out in the dusk that pale piece of ice swept over by the white-crested waves.

Józef Konrad had now completed his necessary four years sea time and gained valuable experience as a seaman, including a voyage around the world. On his return to London, he was sufficiently confident of his seamanship and his knowledge of the English language to sit the examination for his second mate's certificate in June 1880. In the British merchant marine, an officer needs to obtain his second mate, first mate and then master's ticket if he is to command a ship. At that time the Marine Board examinations took place at the St Katherine Docks House on Tower Hill. The elderly and cold-eyed assessor would have taken the time to assure himself that this unusual candidate had really served his four years of sea-time, especially in the French ships as claimed. Under continued questioning the youthful candidate needed to clearly explain how he would tack a fully rigged sailing ship or what he would do to haul off a lee shore that suddenly appeared out of the fog! Conrad found the ordeal severe and a character in his novel *Chance* writes of the assessor:

> Greatly reassured by his apparent benevolence, I had at first been very alert in my answers. But at length the feeling of my brain getting addled crept upon me. And still the passionless process went on, with a sense of untold ages having been spent already on mere preliminaries. And then I got frightened … This ancient person, I said to myself, terrified, is so near his grave that he must have lost all sense of time. He is considering this examination in terms of eternity. It is all very well for him. His race is run. But I may find myself coming out of this room into the world of men, a stranger, friendless, forgotten by my very landlady, even were I able after this endless experience to remember the way to my hired home.

The assessor kept Konrad for an hour and a half in the examination chamber and then suddenly said "You will do!" and pushed a blue slip across the table. In what he remembers as the finest day in his life Konrad describes how he then floated down the stairs and emerged from the main entrance as a fully fledged second mate. When his uncle Thaddeus heard this news, he was equally delighted, and his congratulatory letter began:

Firstly, Dear Sir, you have proved to our country and your own people that you have not eaten your bread in the world for four years in vain. Secondly, that you have succeeded in overcoming the difficulties that arise from the language itself and from your difficult position as a foreigner without any patronage to support you ... Now we need, work and endurance, endurance and work.

By this time the British Merchant Navy was the most powerful commercial entity in the world and British shipowners controlled about seventy percent of world trade. Konrad had now earned the right to serve as an officer, importantly he had completed his examination in the English language and henceforward he would use it with increasing assurance. He would now sail as a British merchant seaman under the Red Ensign, and he wrote: 'The Red Ensign – the symbolic, protecting, warm bit of bunting flung wide upon the seas, and destined for so many years to be the only roof over my head.'

With his certificate in hand, Konrad now needed to find a ship and in his book *Chance* he describes how his character went around all the shipowners' offices in London where some junior clerk would supply him with application forms which he took home to complete and then posted in the nearest pillar box. And that was all that ever came of it. In his own words, he might as well have dropped them all properly addressed and stamped into the sewer grating. There were many shipping lines based in London, but without influence it was unlikely he would be considered for any vacancy that might arise. There was however one unorthodox way of going to sea which was known as the 'pier-head jump'. It was not unusual for an out-of-work seaman to be hanging about near the pier head, with his papers in his pocket, ready to fill a berth at the last minute if a member of the crew went missing or was sick. But it was very rare for a watchkeeping officer to be replaced in that manner. One solution to Konrad's problem was to use an agent or a fixer; however, he describes how he met a former shipmate who suggested he go straight to the shipping office and try to speak directly to a personal contact he had there. In his novel *Chance*, he describes his character breaking the rules by entering the shipping office through a door marked 'Private' and presenting himself directly to the shipping master. Just then, a ship's captain enters the office and the protagonist is asked to wait while the following conversation ensues:

'I have been expecting you in every moment to fetch away your Articles, Captain. Here they are all ready for you.'

'No, they aren't ready worse luck. I've got to ask you to strike out my second officer. He got himself knocked down by a draft horse van while crossing the road outside the dock gate, as if he had neither eyes nor ears. And the ship ready to leave the dock at six o'clock tomorrow morning!'

'We must then take his name off.'

'What am I to do? This office closes at four o'clock. I can't find a man in half an hour. Even if I managed to lay hold of someone ready to ship at such short notice I couldn't ship him regularly here – could I?'

'I don't know whether I ought to tell you that I know of a disengaged second mate at hand.'

'Do you mean you have got him here?'

'Yes and he will sleep on board tonight.'

'I'll take your young friend willingly, Mr Powell. If you let him sign on at once I'll take the Articles away with me now.'

Presumably, Konrad used this very same method to join the *Loch Etive*, which was bound to Australia for a cargo of wool. Its captain promoted his third mate to second mate and made Konrad his new third mate. This position was as a spare watchkeeper, to stand in when necessary, but he would never get to be in charge of a watch himself. Most sailing ship crews were divided into two watches, one headed by the mate and the other by the second mate. The day was divided into six watches of four hours, which starting at midnight were 12 to 4, 4 to 8, 8 to 12, 12 to 4, the 'dog watch' of 4 to 6 and then 6 to 8, and 8 to 12. The uneven number of watches meant a day-to-day rotation of the working hours for the crew of the first and second mates. The captain did not usually stand watch but took command when he pleased or when it was necessary such as in heavy weather, carrying out complex manoeuvres or entering or leaving port. During the voyage the second mate fell ill and Konrad was promoted to 'officer of the watch' which would have been good experience for him in his first voyage as a junior officer on a British ship.

The Glasgow Lochs were known as smart clippers, but the *Loch Etive* was a newer version with rather fuller lines, forced upon her owners to permit the stowage of bulkier cargo on her 'general out, wool home' voyages to Australia. After Konrad joined the ship, she sailed down the Thames, past Kent, through the Channel, down the Atlantic, past the Cape of Good Hope and into the gales of the Roaring Forties that led to Australia. The *Loch Etive*'s voyage lasted ninety-four days. They arrived in Sydney without incident and after loading with wool and a stormy voyage home they were back in London by April 1881.

3
Voyage of the *Highland Forest*, 1887

I call to mind a winter landscape in Amsterdam – a flat foreground of waste land, with here and there stacks of timber, like the huts of a camp of some very miserable tribe; the long stretch of the Handelskade; cold, stone-faced quays, with the snow-sprinkled ground and the hard, frozen water of the canal, in which were set ships one behind another with their frosty mooring-ropes hanging slack and their decks idle and deserted. Because, as the master stevedore informed me, their cargoes were frozen-in up-country on barges.

Joseph Conrad, *The Mirror of the Sea*

Konrad then spent a long break from the sea and considered various business opportunities including whaling as a commercial venture before gaining his first mate's certificate in December 1884 and he writes of his assessor in *A Personal Record*:

He kept inscrutably silent for a moment, and then, placing

me in a ship of certain size at sea, under certain conditions of weather, season, and locality - all very clear and precise - ordered me to execute a certain manoeuvre. Before I was halfway through it he did some material damage to the ship. Directly I had grappled with that difficulty he caused another to present itself, and when that too was met he struck another ship before me, creating a very dangerous situation. I felt slightly outraged by this ingenuity in piling up trouble upon a man.

'I wouldn't have got into that mess,' I suggested mildly. 'I could have seen that ship before.'

He never slurred the least bit.

'No you couldn't. The weather's thick.'

'Oh! I didn't know,' I apologised blankly.

Declared passed, Konrad hastily exited the room, mentally bracing himself for the possibility of facing the assessor again in another year or more, should he decide to pursue the master's certificate.

In 1885, Konrad made another voyage to the Far East, sailing from South Wales in the *Tilkhurst* with a full cargo of coal for Singapore. The vessel stayed a month in Singapore unloading cargo and then preparing for an onward voyage to Calcutta to load jute for Dundee. The *Tilkhurst* arrived in Dundee after a year and a few days at sea. Konrad had thus served his twelve months as a first mate and a minimum six years of sea time, and began to prepare himself for the final examination of his merchant navy career: his master's ticket.

Although he would not necessarily gain a command immediately, he had served the necessary sea time and it was prudent for the first mate to be prepared for command as this could be sprung on him at any time. Three months later he obtained his Certificate of Competency as Master in the British Merchant Marine. When Konrad completed the ordeal of his examination, the assessor pushed the signed blue slip across the desk and concluded by telling him that he should go into steam:

'You will go into steam presently. Everybody goes into steam'.

There he was wrong. I never went into steam – not really. If only I live long enough I shall become a bizarre relic of a dead barbarism, a sort of monstrous antiquity, the only seaman of the dark ages who had never gone into steam – not really.

It was a fact that he was now a British master mariner and had been able to forge his own life outside of Poland. He recalled the difficulties he had as a boy in trying to explain his desire to go to sea, and as he wrote in *A Personal Record*:

I had vindicated myself from what had been cried upon as a stupid obstinacy or a fantastic caprice. I don't mean to say that a whole country had been convulsed by my desire to go to sea. But for a boy between fifteen and sixteen, sensitive enough, in all conscience, the commotion of his little world had seemed a very considerable thing indeed.

So considerable that, absurdly enough, the echoes of it linger to this day. I catch myself in hours of solitude and retrospect meeting arguments and charges made thirty-five years ago by voices now forever still; finding things to say that an assailed boy could not have found, simply because of the mysteriousness of his impulses to himself. I understood no more than the people who called upon me to explain myself. There was no precedent. I verily believe mine was the only case of a boy of my nationality and antecedents taking a, so to speak, standing jump out of his racial surroundings and associations.

Konrad then arranged to travel to Czechoslovakia and the fashionable spa resort of Marienbad to meet his uncle, Thadeus Bobrowski, who had gone there for a water cure. The town, surrounded by green mountains, a mosaic of parks and noble houses, would have made a delightful change from his life at sea. They had not seen each other for the twelve years since Konrad had left Poland and no doubt they discussed Konrad's residency status and his application for British citizenship, as the pair could not meet in safety on Russian soil until this matter was settled.

Just a few months later, on 19 August 1886, and eight years after his arrival in Lowestoft, Józef Teodor Konrad Korzeniowski, 'subject of the Russian Empire, of the age of twenty-nine years, mariner, unmarried', obtained a certificate of British naturalisation. A few weeks later he received a letter from his uncle Thaddeus, 'I rejoice from the bottom of my heart that you have settled the matter of your naturalisation, and I clasp my Englishman, as well as my nephew, to my breast.' Konrad became a British citizen at a time when the British Empire dominated the world economically and politically and when nationalist and imperialist feelings ran high. This gave him a sense of security which he had never had in his difficult early life. He paid homage to this 'national spirit' in the last pages of *The Mirror of the Sea* when he wrote:

In this ceaseless rush of shadows and shades, that, like the fantastic forms of clouds cast darkly upon the waters on a windy day, fly past us to fall headlong below the hard edge of an implacable horizon, we must turn to the national spirit, which, superior in its force and continuity to good and evil fortune, can alone give us the feeling of an enduring existence and of invincible power against the fates.

His next voyage to the Far East was in February 1887 when Konrad signed on as first mate of the *Highland Forest*, a three-masted barque of a little over one thousand tons lying in the port of Amsterdam at the Oostelijike Handelskade (Eastern Trade Quay). She was waiting to load general cargo for a voyage to the Dutch East Indies and the port of Semarang on the north coast of Java. It was a very severe winter and when Konrad arrived in Amsterdam the port was ice-bound.

A new captain for the *Highland Forest* had not yet been appointed and Konrad, to his obvious delight, found himself in charge of the ship for several weeks. He wrote that no man appointed as chief mate for the first time in his life would have let that tenacious Dutch winter penetrate his heart. He describes how he would get up early, for no reason whatsoever, except that he was in sole charge. He could not forget the fact of his elevation for five consecutive minutes. He fancied it kept him warm, even in his slumbers, much warmer than the high pile of blankets, which positively crackled with frost as he threw them off in the morning. Even the ink froze in his inkwell and in the evenings he would escape to a warm and comfortable coffee-room in the Hotel Krasnapolsky. The room was an immense place, lofty, gilded, upholstered in red plush, full of electric lights, and so thoroughly heated that even the marble tables felt warm to the touch. Here he would write to the owners in Glasgow that there was no prospect of any cargo coming until spring, before summoning the will to return to his frozen ship and his freezing cabin.

Almost every morning a letter from the owners would arrive, directing him to go to the charterers and clamour for the ship's cargo; to threaten them with the heaviest penalties of demurrage; to demand that this assortment of varied merchandise, frozen fast in a landscape of ice and windmills somewhere up-country, should be put on rail instantly and sent to the ship in regular quantities daily. After drinking some hot coffee he would go ashore, dressed like an Arctic explorer setting off on a sledge journey towards the North Pole, and roll shivering in a tramcar into the heart of Amsterdam to meet with a Mr Hudig of Hudig & Blokhuyzen:

He was a big, swarthy Netherlander, with black moustaches and a bold glance. He always began by shoving me into a chair before I had time to open my mouth, gave me cordially a large cigar, and in excellent English would start to talk everlastingly about the phenomenal severity of the weather. It was impossible to threaten a man who, though he possessed the language perfectly, seemed incapable of understanding any phrase pronounced in a tone of remonstrance or discontent. As to quarrelling with him, it would have been stupid. The weather was too bitter for that. His office was so warm, his fire so bright, his sides shook so heartily with laughter, that I experienced always a great difficulty in making up my mind to reach for my hat.

In time, the cargo started arriving by train and then by canal boats and barges pushing through the icy waters. This was the first loading of general cargo for which Konrad was responsible, and the loading of boxes, crates, machinery and bales of all different sizes, weight and capacities presented him with a complicated stowage feat. If he loaded the weight too high then the ship would roll heavily and if he loaded the weight too low the ship would jerk and shudder as it hit the waves. Each ship had its own idiosyncrasies and the best loading advice would always come from one of the ship's former crew, but without having any prior knowledge of the ship's particular sailing characteristics Konrad was on his own. He loaded the ship according to textbook advice which was to put two-thirds of the cargo below the beams and one-third above the beams near the top of the hold.

After the loading was complete, and on the eve of their departure, a stranger in a black bowler and short drab overcoat appeared on the quay. The stranger walked up and down, absorbed in marked contemplation of the ship's fore and aft trim, he squatted on his heels in the slush at the very edge of the quay to peer at the draught of water under the hull. It was the new captain, John McWhirr, who had in fact been the previous first mate on the *Highland Forest* and as described by Conrad:

I said to myself, 'This is the captain.' And presently I descried his luggage coming along – a real sailor's chest, carried by means of rope-beckets between two men, with a couple of leather portmanteaus and a roll of charts sheeted in canvas piled upon the lid. The sudden, spontaneous agility with which he bounded aboard right off the rail afforded me the first glimpse of his real character. Without further preliminaries than a friendly nod, he addressed me: 'You have got her pretty well in her fore and aft trim. Now, what about your weights?'

I told him I had managed to keep the weight sufficiently well up, as I thought, with one-third of the whole being in the upper part 'above the beams,' according to the textbook advice. He whistled 'Phew!' scrutinising me from head to foot. A sort of smiling vexation was visible on his ruddy face. 'Well, we shall have a lively time of it this passage, I bet,' he said.

The passage to the East Indies was a non-stop voyage of seven and a half thousand miles for the *Highland Forest*. First down the Atlantic and around the Cape of Good Hope, then bearing south towards the wild westerlies of the Roaring Forties for almost four thousand miles before turning north towards the Sunda Straits between Java and Sumatra. *The Highland Forest* tended towards stiffness, it needed a lot more cargo stowed above the beams and so the outcome of Konrad's loading was an extremely uncomfortable voyage in which the ship rolled excessively:

> Running before the gales of high latitudes, she made our life a burden to us. There were days when nothing would keep even on the swing-tables, when there was no position where you could fix yourself so as not to feel a constant strain upon all the muscles of your body. She rolled and rolled with an awful dislodging jerk and that dizzily fast sweep of her masts on every swing. It was a wonder that the men sent aloft were not flung off the yards, the yards not flung off the masts, the masts not flung overboard. The captain in his armchair, holding on grimly at the head of the table, with the soup-tureen rolling on one side of the cabin and the steward sprawling on the other, would observe, looking at me: 'That's your one-third above the beams. The only thing that surprises me is that the sticks have stuck to her all this time.'

As Conrad wrote in *The Mirror of the Sea*, it was only poetic justice that the chief mate who had made such a mistake – perhaps a half-excusable one – about the distribution of his ship's cargo should pay the penalty. A piece of one of the minor spars did carry away, flew against Konrad's back and sent him sliding on his face along the main deck for a considerable distance. Conrad describes in fictional terms the results of this accident in his book *Lord Jim*:

> Jim, disabled by a falling spar at the beginning of a week of which his Scottish captain used to say afterwards, 'Man! it's a pairfect meeracle to me how he lived through it!' spent many days stretched on his back, dazed, battered, hopeless, and tormented as if at the bottom of an abyss of unrest. He did not care what the end would be, and in his lucid moments overvalued his indifference. The danger, when not seen, has the imperfect vagueness of human thought. The fear grows shadowy; and imagination, the enemy of men, the father of all terrors, unstimulated, sinks to rest in the dullness of exhausted emotion. Jim saw nothing but the disorder of his tossed cabin. He lay there battened down in the midst of a small devastation, and felt secretly glad he had not to go on deck.

The port of Semarang lay on the north coast of Java and gave access to the dense population of Central Java, and most of the general cargo unloaded would be to service the vast sugar, tobacco and coffee plantations that the Dutch had established there. After the *Highland Forest* had unloaded her cargo, Konrad's injuries persisted and he reported to the Dutch doctor there that he was experiencing 'inexplicable periods of powerlessness and sudden accesses of mysterious pain.' A serious accident of some sort was an accepted part of a seaman's life, particularly in an ocean-going square rigger and the doctor told him the injury may be serious for his whole life. 'You must leave your ship and you must be quite silent for three months.'

Konrad was discharged from the *Highland Forest* on 18 July 1887 and sent on the next ship for hospitalisation in Singapore. Here he was registered at the European hospital as a 'Distressed British Seaman' to recover from his injury. While sweating in his hospital bed it seemed impossible to recall the dreadful cold and snow of Amsterdam, while looking at the fronds of the tropical palm trees tossing and rustling outside his window. He lyrically describes his hospital experience in *Lord Jim*:

There were only two other patients in the white men's ward: the purser of a gunboat, who had broken his leg falling down a hatchway; and a kind of railway contractor from a neighbouring province, afflicted by some mysterious tropical disease, who held the doctor for an ass, and indulged in secret debaucheries of a patent medicine which his Tamil servant used to smuggle in with unwearied devotion. They told each other the story of their lives, played cards a little, or, yawning and in pyjamas, lounged through the day in easy-chairs without saying a word. The hospital stood on a hill, and a gentle breeze entering through the windows, always flung wide open, brought into the bare room the softness of the sky, the languor of the earth, the bewitching breath of the Eastern waters. There were perfumes in it, suggestions of infinite repose, the gift of endless dreams. Jim looked

every day over the thickets of gardens, beyond the roofs
of the town, over the fronds of palms growing on the
shore, at that roadstead which is a thoroughfare to the
East, at the roadstead dotted by garlanded islets, lighted
by festal sunshine, its ships like toys, its brilliant activity
resembling a holiday pageant, with the eternal serenity
of the Eastern sky overhead and the smiling peace of the
Eastern seas possessing the space as far as the horizon.

As soon as he could walk without a stick, Konrad moved out
of the hospital for a further period of rehabilitation and to look
for the possibility of a berth back to England. Nothing offered
just then, and while waiting he spent time with the other seamen
in the port. He stayed in Sailors' Home which was located in
the European quarter on the east side of the Singapore River and
directly behind St Andrew's Cathedral. It was what he describes
in *The Shadow-Line* as a large bungalow with a wide verandah,
a curiously suburban-looking garden of bushes and a few trees
between the building and the street.

Once he had fully recovered, Konrad would walk daily
from Sailors' Home towards the port buildings, past the white
spire of the cathedral, past the frontages of the new government
buildings, past the famous Hotel de l'Europe and along the shaded
Esplanade with its enormous trees towards the Singapore River,
the Cavenagh Bridge and the Harbour Office with its portal of
dressed white stone above a flight of white steps, to look for a
passage home.

4

The Founding of Singapore

> Singapore at that time was like the sun when it has
> just risen, waxing stronger and stronger as it gets higher
> and higher ... I am astonished to see how markedly the
> world is changing. A new world is being created, the old
> world destroyed. The very jungle becomes settled district
> and elsewhere a settlement reverts to jungle.
>
> Abdullah bin Abdul Kadir, *Hikayat Abdullah*, 1849

After his arrival in Singapore, Konrad was amazed to learn that this prosperous and bustling settlement had been founded only seventy years earlier in February 1819.

Major William Farquhar, the British Resident in Malacca from 1803 to 1818, sailed south from Penang in January 1819 with the English East India Company ships *Nearchus*, the *Mercury,* the brig *Ganges* and a small schooner, *Enterprise,* to claim a site for a British settlement in the region of the Riau Islands. Stamford Raffles had orders to first settle a dynastic dispute in Aceh, but managed to ignore his orders and slipped out of Penang that evening on the *Indiana* hoping to join Farquhar in claiming a site for a British settlement. In the Malacca Strait, the fleet met up with two armed survey ships of the English East India Company, the *Discovery* and the *Investigator,* who were conducting a hydrographic survey of the Strait.

William Farquhar, who knew the Strait well, had suggested Carimon Island as a likely place for a settlement because the British had some prior claim, but they found the island was completely covered in jungle and after three days of surveying the coastline, no suitable harbour could be found. The next possibility was the Johor River Estuary, and it was the hydrographer Captain Daniel Ross who suggested that the small fleet stop at the mouth of the Singapore River enroute to Johor:

> Captain Ross pointed out on the chart a spot he considered more eligible in point of harbour cleared of jungle and advantageous for trade, to the north east of St. Johns Island which he had observed on a passage to China, it was agreed we should in the morning get under way and examine this port before deciding on any other.

The small fleet of seven ships reached Singapore Island on the morning of 29 January 1819. They were looking for the mouth of the Singapore River which was hidden behind a small headland. Here they found a good safe anchorage close to the shore, a basin at the mouth of the river that was an ideal harbour for small cargo boats and there was plenty of wood and fresh water. Raffles wrote in his official despatch:

The island of Singapore, independently of the straits and harbour of Johor, which it both forms and commands, has, on its southern shores, and by means of several smaller islands which lie off it, excellent anchorage and smaller harbours, and seems in every respect most peculiarly adapted for our object. Its position in the Straits of Singapore is far more convenient and commanding than even Riau, for our China trade passing down the Straits of Malacca, and every native vessel that sails through the Straits of Riau must pass in sight of it.

They were pleased to see a flat area to the northeast of the river cleared of jungle and with a small settlement of Malay houses. Temenggong Abdu'r-Rahman lived in one of the larger houses; he came out to welcome his old friend William Farquhar and invited them inside his house. Introduced to Stamford Raffles, he told them of the current dispute within the Johor-Riau Sultanate. In 1810 Sultan Mahmud Shah of Johor died. His eldest son, Tengku Long, was his successor; however, the powerful Bugis faction in the Johor-Riau court exploited Tengku Long's absence at his wedding in Pahang to declare his more compliant younger brother Tungku Abdu'r-Rahman as sultan.

William Farquhar and Stamford Raffles persuaded the temenggong of the advantage of a British settlement and factory in Singapore. He signed a provisional agreement with them before sending a messenger to Tengku Long at Tanjung Pinang with the news that a British fleet was in Singapore and was willing to recognise him as the rightful Sultan of Johor. Tengku Long, as the 'legitimate successor to the empire of Johor' saw an agreement with the British as an opportunity to counter the Bugis and his younger brother.

The following day the lookout sighted a Malay war *prahu* approaching Singapore flying the yellow flag of Malay royalty. Tengku Long was approaching. Greeted by the temenggong and Colonel Farquhar, he then dressed in his regal attire before boarding the *Indiana* to receive a royal welcome. The meeting with Sir Stamford Raffles is described some decades later in the Bugis history, the *Tufat al-Nafis*:

The Temenggong ... then sent Raja Ambung to Riau to fetch Tengku Long, and when Raja Ambung met Tengku Long he informed him of all the secret plans of Mr Raffles, Colonel Farquhar and the Temenggong. Tengku Long was amenable and when night fell he set sail with Raja Ambung for Singapore. When he arrived on 6 February 1819, the Temenggong and Colonel Farquhar took him aboard the warship to meet Mr Raffles, who honoured Tengku Long in the way kings are honoured, by firing the cannon, beating drums and so forth. Afterwards he was taken below and given a chair sitting beside Mr Raffles and Colonel Farquhar. Mr Raffles told him everything, using courteous words, advising him, and paying him delicate compliments. And Tengku Long agreed to whatever Mr Raffles proposed, and so after the affair was settled the discussions and agreements were put into effect.

The treaty gave the British the right to set up a factory in Singapore for the payment of five thousand Spanish dollars a year to the sultan and three thousand Spanish dollars a year to the temenggong. The sultan retained the right to the land, even within the bounds of the British factory, and was entitled to one half of the duties which might be levied on the port.

Significantly Tengku Long did not immediately lay claim to the throne of Johor, as this would have invited a confrontation between himself and his younger brother. In the eyes of the Riau court, he had been installed as Sultan Husain Syah, son of the late Sultan Mahmud Syah, in the state of Singapore and all its subject territories.

Raffles wrote up his official Proclamation:

A Treaty having this day been concluded between the British Government and the native authorities, and a British Establishment having been in consequence founded at Singapore. The Honourable Sir T.S. Raffles, Lieutenant–Governor of Bencoolen and its dependencies, Agent to the Governor-General, is pleased to certify the appointment by the Supreme Government, of Major William Farquhar of the Madras Engineers to be Resident and to command the troops at Singapore and its dependencies, and all persons are hereby directed to obey Major Farquhar accordingly. It is further notified that the Residency of Singapore has been placed under the Government of Fort Marlborough, and is to be considered a dependency thereof; of which all persons concerned are desired to take notice.

Dated at Singapore this 6th day of February 1819.

To undercut its main competitor, the Dutch East India Company based in Batavia, the English East India Company designated Singapore as a free port with no tariffs and trade restrictions. Raffles said that he was interested in trade not territory, and one of the first people to comment on the trading opportunities in Singapore was the twenty-two-year-old James Matheson, making his second visit to China as cargo officer on the opium ship *Marquis of Hastings,* who wrote in 1819:

> I have formed the highest opinion of Singapore as a place of trade. Its principal staple article at the moment is tin, for which there is a melting house belonging to the Sultan of Johor ... as yet however no trade can be carried out to any great extent there being no merchants to deal with; this is a disadvantage which, as there are no duties or port charges, will soon vanish. I am of the opinion that a person settling here for a few months with a few thousand dollars as a circulating medium might carry on business to a great advantage.

A sketch map of Singapore made only a few years after the founding of the settlement shows how quickly it had developed. The entrance to the river was protected by a rocky point and it is from opposite here that people were ferried across the river. Roads had been laid out and warehouses and godowns were being erected on both sides of the river. Districts had already established with the Chinese Kampong shown on the west side of the river, the government area on the east bank of the river and up to the freshwater river which follows present-day Stamford Road. Pencilled writing on the sketch map indicates that north of this river was part of the European town, followed by the Malay quarter and the residence of the sultan at Kampong Glam. A gun battery to defend the settlement was placed in front of the parade ground, and a brick kiln had been established on the upper part of the Singapore River to provide building material for the rapidly expanding settlement. The area shown on the sketch as the Old Lines of Singapore represented ancient embankments built around the 'Forbidden Hill' – so called because of its religious and historic links to the ancient settlement of Singapore and the tombs of former Malay kings buried there.

Singapore would inherit the position of the pre-eminent trading city in the region after Malacca, Johor, Batavia and Tanjung Pinang. William Farquhar was able to write in 1820, and only one year after its founding:

Nothing can possibly exceed the rising trade and general prosperity of this infant colony; indeed to look at the harbour right now, where upwards of twenty junks, three of which are from China, and two from Cochin China, the rest from Siam and other quarters, are at anchor, besides ships, brigs, prows etc. etc., a person would exclaim, Surely this cannot be an establishment of twelve months standing! ... In short, this settlement bids fair to become the emporium of Eastern trade, and in time may even surpass Batavia itself.

Sir Stamford Raffles and Lady Sophia arrived from Fort Marlborough at Bencoolen in Sumatra on their last visit to Singapore on 10 October 1822. Sick and fatigued, Raffles' wife Sophia desperately ill, and three of his children buried in Bencoolen, his one last imperative was to bring order, law and a just administration to what he saw as the chaos of Singapore. Everything was wrong! The town had not been built according to his plan. No code of law for the settlement had been drawn up, the defences were incomplete, and the swamp on which the business quarter was to stand had not been filled in. If Farquhar opposed him, then Farquhar must go! Whoever stood in his way must be removed!

Raffles main grievance was that his instructions to reserve land on the east bank of the Singapore River exclusively for the government had not been followed. To set matters right Raffles formed a Town Committee and on 4th November issued a detailed list of instructions covering every aspect of Singapore's future development. Raffles appointed Lieutenant Phillip Jackson with the task of drawing up a town plan based on Raffles' instructions to the Town Committee. Vast gangs of labour – Malay, Indian and Chinese – moved mountains to fill in the swampy land west of the river, and a stone wall was constructed along the riverside. Roads were made according to Raffles' original plan, markets were laid out, resettlement of Malays and the Chinese into the replanned Kampong Glam and Chinatown was undertaken, and land office staff were engaged to issue proper land titles. A miracle was performed, which required ruthless action and the deep pockets of the English East India Company – at least until they sent Raffles the bill.

Stamford Raffles was ill, periodically suffering from blinding headaches and nausea in what was then described as 'brain fever'. In this condition he expressed a wish to be buried near the Keramat Iskandar Shah which was located near Government Hill (present-day Fort Canning). Raffles wrote that 'should I die in Singapore, my bones will have the honour of mixing with the ashes of the Malayan Kings.'

The clash of temperaments between Raffles and Farquhar, the co-founders of Singapore, finally came to a head on 1 May 1823 when Raffles churlishly dismissed Farquhar from office just as his term was about to end. Farquhar's successor, Dr John Crawfurd, arrived on the 27th of the same month and immediately took up his new office as Resident of Singapore.

The following month, Raffles left Singapore for the last time. The island's future was no longer uncertain. He had stamped his ambition on the settlement, and Abdullah bin Abdul Kadir wrote in his *Hikayat Abdullah*:

Mr Raffles and his Lady embarked, followed by hundreds of people of all races, myself among the rest, as far as the ship: and when they had ascended the ship's side and the crew were raising the anchor Mr Raffles called me to him and I went into his cabin where I observed that he was flushed as if he had been wiping his tears. He told me to return and not be distressed 'If it is to be, I will see you again.' His Lady now came and gave me twenty-five dollars, saying 'I give these to your children in Malacca,' and when I heard that my heart burned the more by this act of grace. I thanked her very much, clasping them by the hand in tears, and then descended to my sampan and when I had been off some distance I turned around and saw Mr Raffles looking out of the window, when I again saluted him. He raised his hand to me. This was just as the sails were being hoisted; and the vessel sailed.

In December 1823 the Dutch colonial minister, Anton Reinhard Falk, during his negotiations with Lord Castlereagh, the foreign secretary for Great Britain, suggested drawing a line down the Malacca Strait which would divide the region between the Dutch and the British. The Anglo-Dutch Treaty of 1824, also known as the Treaty of London, re-assigned Malacca to Britain in exchange for the Dutch receiving the British territory of Bencoolen in Sumatra. The entire Malay world was split in two with Sumatra, the Riau islands and eastern Borneo under Dutch rule, and the Malay Peninsula, Singapore and western Borneo under British rule, eventually leading to the founding of three separate countries, Indonesia, Malaysia and Singapore. The British motivation for signing the Treaty of London was that the Netherlands would withdraw its opposition to the British occupation of Singapore. In return the British agreed not to establish any settlement or sign any treaties with any of the Riau Islands south of the Strait of Singapore, such as

Carimon, Batam or Bintan.

The new Resident of Singapore, John Crawfurd, joined the English East India Company in 1803 as a medical officer and had served under Raffles when he was Governor of Java. Crawfurd recognised that the 1819 treaty with Sultan Husain Syah amounted to little more than permission for the formation of a British settlement along two miles of shore and inland to the extent of a cannon shot. There was in reality no territorial concession giving a legal right of legislation. The only law that could have existed was the Malay code and the sultan was considered to be the proprietor of the land, even within the bounds of the British settlement.

It was Crawfurd who created the conditions whereby Sultan Husain Syah was forced to give full control of Singapore to the English East India Company. He first questioned the cash payments made to the sultan and the temenggong in the 1819 treaty, saying that they had never been approved by Calcutta, and the not so Honourable Company demanded repayment. After five years of payments this was a huge sum of money which the sultan was clearly unable to pay. This demand was unethical and immoral, but the geopolitical balance had changed in favour of the British. The Treaty of London meant Britain no longer needed the support of the Malay sultans of Johor, Singapore or Riau to counter the Dutch. Sultan Husain Syah and Temenggong Abdu'r-Rahman had suddenly lost their importance to the English East India Company. In June 1824, Crawford stopped all payments to the sultan and the temenggong, and inferred that their debts could be cleared by signing a new treaty with the English East India

Company. In August 1824, Sultan Husain Syah and Temenggong Abdu'r-Rahman were driven up to Government Hill for a meeting with the British Resident. This meeting is described in the *Hikayat Abdullah*, written by Raffles' former Malay scribe Abdullah bin Abdul Kadir:

> On arrival they were greeted by Mr Crawfurd and invited into his house where they sat down. After they had been seated for a few moments, Mr Crawfurd said, 'Is it true that Your Highness is ready to accede to the wishes of the Governor-General?' The Sultan said 'It is true.' Then Mr Crawfurd asked the Temenggong who also gave his assent. After that Mr Crawfurd took two pieces of parchment out of his writing-box saying, "This document is to certify that I, Sultan Husain Shah ibn Al-Marhum Sultan Mahmud Shah, ruler of the Kingdoms of Johor and Pahang, whose sovereignty extends over the settlement of Singapore, do sincerely declare in this Treaty of my own free will I have ceded this Settlement of Singapore and all authority over it to the English East India Company.

In return, the sultan received 33,200 Spanish silver dollars and the temenggong the sum of 26,800 Spanish silver dollars, and an increase in their annual stipends to 15,600 and 8,400 Spanish silver dollars respectively. Sultan Husain Mahmud Shah had his court in the coastal settlement known as Kampong Glam which was east of the European town, between the Arab kampong and the Bugis kampong. His subjects traditionally traded in maritime goods from the Riau islands, supported by some occasional piracy. Here the Malays, Orang Laut and Bugis could anchor their vessels in the shallow water in front of Kampong Glam or access the deeper water of the Kallang River Basin to build their ships and unload their goods. Early maps of Singapore show the location of the sultan's compound and residence with the mosque behind it. The first Sultan Mosque was built in Kampong Glam in 1824 with funds of three thousand Spanish dollars contributed by the English East India Company. The original sultan's residence, built of timber with a thatched attap roof, was rebuilt in 1840 by his grandson in the European Palladian style (the present-day Malay Heritage Centre). Despite the payments made to him by the English East India Company, Sultan Husain Mahmud Shah died in poverty and exile in Malacca in 1835 and is buried there at the Tranquera Mosque.

A white polymarble copy of Thomas Woolner's original 1887 bronze statue of Sir Thomas Stamford Raffles stands where he and William Farquhar first landed on the north bank of the Singapore River. Raffles, in double life-size, stands with his arms across his chest, more in a pensive than a heroic mode, and the plaque reads:

On this historic site, Sir Thomas Stamford Raffles first landed in Singapore on 28th January 1819, and with genius and perception changed the destiny of Singapore from an obscure fishing village to a great seaport and modern metropolis.

Behind his statue and over the river, the huge banking and

commercial buildings of the Central Business District stand as a legacy to Raffles' dream of 'creating a settlement which would become the emporium of Eastern trade and in time may even surpass Batavia itself.'

5

That Great Eastern Port: Singapore

Singapore is the meeting place of many races. The Malays,
though natives of the soil dwell uneasily in towns, and
are few; and it is the Chinese, supple, alert and industrious,
who throng the streets; the dark skinned Tamils walk on
their silent, naked feet, as though they were but brief sojourners
in a strange land, but the Bengalis, sleek and prosperous, are
easy in their surroundings, and self-assured ... and the English in
their topees and white ducks, speeding past in motor cars
or at leisure in their rickshaws wear a nonchalant and careless
air. The rulers of these teeming peoples take their authority
with a smiling unconcern.

Somerset Maugham, 'P&O' (1922)

The main beneficiaries of the new settlement in Singapore were
English traders and their Asian counterparts – the Chinese, Arab,
Malay and Bugis traders who were all attracted to Singapore.
Only three months after its founding, David Napier and his

Penang-born partner Charles Scott set up in Singapore as 'Eastern traders' and built a warehouse on the Singapore River, just by the first bend upstream. The next trader to arrive was Claude Quieros who built a warehouse on the Singapore River next to the English East India Company store. A former sea captain, Mr Alec Laurie Johnston built the town's first landing jetty and secured a prime position for his warehouse near the entrance to the river, which became known as Tanjung Tangkap or the 'Catch All Trade Point'. Next were Graham Mackenzie and then Alexander Guthrie, whose company was to become one of the biggest trading companies in the Far East. Six years later a China trader by the name of Edward Boustead started his company and was described as a far-sighted chap because he and his partners bought some prized land sites and built splendid houses on them.

The Straits Chinese had already started moving to the new settlement from Malacca, Penang, Johor and around the Riau islands. They were now being augmented by immigrant Chinese arriving by junk from Amoy, Canton and other ports along the China coast. These newcomers jostled for work along the waterfront, clearing the jungle or moving dirt to fill in the swampy low ground. Plenty of enterprising Chinese were ready to act as 'middlemen' for the English traders and distribute their goods to the Chinese shopkeepers springing up in Singapore. Bugis traders brought slaves, spices, beeswax, Bugis cotton cloth and coffee from Macassar to Singapore in exchange for iron bars, firearms, gunpowder and opium, and thousands of them would settle in what became known as Kampong Bugis. In the 1830s the Bugis population in Singapore peaked at around two thousand people when the Bugis merchants had a virtual monopoly over trade with the eastern islands of the Indonesian archipelago. The growing dominance of Western ships and steamers increased competition for the Bugis traders operating out of Singapore and their role was gradually reduced.

Goods were sold for Spanish silver dollars or bartered for pepper, gambier leaves (used as a brown dye and in leather tanning), cloves, nutmeg, tin and gold dust to be delivered and stored in warehouses awaiting shipment to London, Calcutta or Canton. Set squarely on the main west-east and east-west shipping routes across the Orient, the Eastern port referred to in Joseph Conrad's books is of course Singapore, even though he never uses that name to describe the port. The material for Conrad's eastern novels was all around him. Singapore was to be the 'Eastern port' of *Lord Jim*, *The End of the Tether* and *The Shadow-Line*. It was a thriving port with a busy harbour and a city containing an exciting mixture of races. Hundreds of ships lay bow to stern in the roadstead waiting to be offloaded onto thousands of lighters, and their crews to be brought ashore by thousands of sampans, all manned by thousands of Chinese. Conrad describes the ships in the harbour with the Riau Islands in the background in his book *The End of the Tether*:

It was a terraced shore, and beyond, upon the level expanse, profound and glistening like the gaze of a dark-blue eye, an oblique band of stippled purple lengthened itself indefinitely through the gap between a couple of verdant twin islets. The masts and spars of a few ships far away, hull down in the outer roads, sprang straight from the water in a fine maze of rosy lines pencilled on the clear shadow of the eastern board.

The arrival on 4 August 1845 of the first P&O steamer, the *Lady Mary Wood*, a paddle-wheel steamer of 556 tonnes signalled the twilight of the dense fleet of sailing ships in Singapore harbour. She took forty-one days to steam from London around the Cape of Good Hope and then to Ceylon, Calcutta, Penang and Singapore before continuing to Hong Kong. In 1851 P&O secured the British government contract to provide full fortnightly steamship service to India, Singapore and China as well as a branch line from Singapore to Australia. Hence, by the following year there were two P&O services to Singapore, the China route and the Australia route. The use of steamships enabled the faster exchange of information between Britain and its far-flung colonies and began to transform the meaning of travel as it brought transient visitors and tourists who would stay in Singapore for up to a month before sailing on to other destinations.

All this changed again when the Suez Canal opened in 1869. This was the beginning of the end for the beautiful sailing clippers and the noble seamen, men like Konrad Korzeniowski, who sailed them. The piercing of the Isthmus of Suez, like the breaking of a dam, let in upon the East a flood of steamships and changed the face of the Eastern seas. According to Joseph Conrad the sea was now a used-up drudge, wrinkled and defaced by the churned-up wakes of brutal propellers, robbed of the enslaving charm of its vastness, stripped of its beauty, of its mystery and of its promise.

He did not hold back in expressing his view of this change when he wrote:

> Then a great pall of smoke sent out by countless steam-boats was spread over the restless mirror of the Infinite. The hand of the engineer tore down the veil of the terrible beauty in order that greedy and faithless landlubbers might pocket dividends. The mystery was destroyed. Like all mysteries, it lived only in the hearts of its worshippers. The hearts changed; the men changed. The once loving and devoted servants went out armed with fire and iron, and conquering the fear of their own hearts became a calculating crowd of cold and exacting masters.

Between 1870 and 1890 the value of exports and imports passing through Singapore nearly tripled, and Singapore boomed as a regional entrepot where half of everything that arrived in the city was off-loaded onto different vessels for delivery to ports on the Malay Peninsula, Borneo and the Dutch East Indies. Alfred Russel Wallace, the famous naturalist, who also became one of the greatest archipelago travellers, arrived in Singapore in 1854 on a P&O steamer and we have his description of the port city from this period:

> Few places are more interesting to a traveller from Europe than the town and the island of Singapore, furnishing as it does, examples of a variety of Eastern races, and of many different religions and modes of life. The government,

the garrison and the chief merchants are English, but the great mass of the population is Chinese, including some of the wealthiest merchants, the agriculturalists of the interior, and most of the mechanics and labourers. The native Malays are usually the fishermen and boatmen, and they form the main body of the police. The Portuguese of Malacca supply a large number of the clerks and smaller merchants. The Klings of Western India are a numerous body of Mohammedans, and with many Arabs, are petty merchants and shop-keepers ... The harbour is crowded with men-of-war and trading vessels of many European nations, and hundreds of Malay praus and Chinese junks, from vessels of several hundred tons burden down to little fishing-boats and passenger sampans; and the town comprises handsome public buildings and churches, Mohammedan mosques, Hindoo temples, Chinese joss-houses, good European houses, massive warehouses, queer old Kling and China bazaars, and long suburbs of Chinese and Malay cottages.

Few would believe it today, but Wallace describes how tigers roamed the jungles of Singapore and would kill on average a Chinaman every day, principally those working in the gambier plantations which are always located in newly cleared jungle on the outskirts of the settlement. Not only were the tigers themselves a threat but also the tiger pits dug to trap them, which were carefully covered with sticks and leaves. Originally, a sharp stake was stuck erect at the bottom of the pit, but after an unfortunate traveller had been killed by falling on one, its use was forbidden.

Along the harbourside and with a view of the ships lined up in the Singapore Roads were the Post Office, Harbour Office, the offices of the ships chandlers and the various shipping agents. In Konrad's time, a rambling two-storey building with a colonnaded façade and shuttered windows stood on the point near the Cavenagh Bridge where Flint Street met Battery Road. It contained the premises of McAlister and Company – ships chandlers, sailmakers, ship brokers and general merchants. A cavernous space which contained every sundry item that a ship needed to put to sea. In the same building was Emmerson's Tiffin, Billiard and Reading Rooms, which drew sailors, merchants and those from the Harbour Office to its daily lunch menu, advertised as Tiffin à la Carte and best described as mulligatawny soup and Malay chicken curry and rice. These men liked the noisy camaraderie of Emmerson's rooms which were filled with tales of ships, sailors, piracy, disasters at sea and the latest rumours.

The location of the present-day Fullerton Hotel was once the site of the former Post Office and Harbour Office of Conrad's time. A memorial to Joseph Conrad stands on the seafront of the hotel and is dedicated to him as a 'British Master Mariner and great English writer who made Singapore and the whole of Southeast Asia better known to the world'. A narrow street led back from the Landing-Place to Commercial Square with a constant stream of Chinese, Malays, Indians, Parsees and Mohammedans moving one way or the other and this street became known as 'Change Alley'. Commercial Square, now known as Raffles Place, was where the banks and commercial houses were located and where the everlasting clink of dollars being counted by their Chinese cashiers could be heard. Behind here was the beginning of Chinatown with its crowded streets and busy shops. The nineteenth-century English naturalist F.W. Burbridge, arriving in Singapore at the start of his Borneo travels, paints a picture of business in Commercial Square in his 1880 journal *The Gardens of the Sun*:

> A morning in the 'Square' gives one a relatively clear insight into the enterprise and trade of Singapore. You hear a good deal about the price of sago or gutta and rice, or about the chartering of steamers or sailing craft, or the freight on home or export goods. You are sure to meet two or three captains of trading steamers, Captain Lingard, perhaps, after one of his trips to the Kutei River away on the southeast of Borneo, and then you will hear something of the rubber-market or of pirates.

Spanning the entrance to the Singapore River, Cavenagh Bridge provided then as it does today one of the most famous views of Singapore, and in Konrad's day Boat Quay was packed with thousands of lighters, tongkangs and sampans bringing goods and people into the river. The crescent of buildings and warehouses along the quay was taken up with the unloading and loading of these boats. Hundreds of coolies unloaded huge crates, casks, boxes and bales of British manufactured goods into the warehouses, to be followed by the loading of bales of gambier, bundles of rattans, bags of tin, bags of sago, tapioca or rice, and bags of pepper and spices for export to foreign markets. Conrad describes this scene in his book *The Rescue*:

> One evening about six months before Lingard's last trip, as they were crossing the short bridge over the canal where native craft lay moored in clusters … Jorgenson pointed out the mass of praus, coasting boats, and sampans that, jammed together in the canal, lay covered with mats and flooded by the cold moonlight, with here and there a dim lantern burning amongst the confusion of high sterns, spars, masts, and lowered sails.

On the north side of Cavenagh Bridge, avenues of large trees ran straight along the Esplanade, cutting each other at diverse angles, columnar below and luxuriant above. Singapore's social elite would promenade daily around the Esplanade to enjoy the cool evening breeze and to see and be seen. Konrad would have witnessed the European ladies of Singapore emerge from their homes and together with their husbands drive in their carriages back and forth along the space that would later be renamed the Padang. This scene was enlivened twice a week by the regimental band, on which occasions women gathered at what was known as Scandal Point to gossip and for their daughters to indulge in a little innocent flirtation. The various married couples would pass and repass the assembled group in their conveyances, and at times they would stop to speak to acquaintances.

The P&O steamships stopped in Alexandria, Port Said, Aden, Columbo and Penang enroute to Singapore and then Hong Kong.

The steamships brought travellers and tourists intent on a tour of Asia and the place to stay in Singapore was the Hotel d'Europe which was located on the corner of High Street and the Esplanade and was renamed Hotel de L'Europe in 1865. It was a palatial building, displaying its white pillared pavilions and surrounded by trim grass plots, which Conrad names in *Lord Jim* as the Malabar Hotel:

> An outward-bound mail-boat had come in that afternoon, and the big dining-room of the hotel was more than half full of people with a-hundred-pounds-round-the-world tickets in their pockets. There were married couples looking domesticated and bored with each other in the midst of their travels; there were small parties and large parties, and lone individuals dining solemnly or feasting boisterously, but all thinking, conversing, joking, or scowling as was their wont at home; and just as intelligently receptive of new impressions as their trunks upstairs. Henceforth they would be labelled as having passed through this and that place, and so would be their luggage. They would cherish this distinction of their persons, and preserve the gummed tickets on their portmanteaus as documentary evidence, as the only permanent trace of their improving enterprise.

In early August 1880 news reached Singapore from Aden of the sinking of the pilgrim ship *Jeddah* carrying 900 Muslim pilgrims to complete the Hajj, whose fate was now unknown.

Days later this was followed by the news that the pilgrims had survived, that the ship had not sunk, but had been abandoned by its captain and crew in absolute violation of the maritime code that they should be the last to leave a sinking ship. The steamship *Jeddah* had left Singapore in July 1880 for Penang to pick up 953 Muslim pilgrims bound for the Mecca. The ship was operated under the name of the Singapore Steamship Company which was owned by Syed Mohsin bin Salleh Al Joffree. There were seven European officers on board including Captain Clark, the first mate, the second mate, as well as the chief, second and third engineers. On 10 August the news report told how the vessel had sunk with the only survivors being the European crew and it read:

Aden: August 10, 1880

The steamer *Jeddah* of Singapore, bound for Jeddah, with 953 pilgrims on board, foundered off Cape Guardafui on the 8th inst. All on board perished, excepting the captain, his wife, the chief officer, the chief engineer, the assistant engineer, and 16 natives. The survivors were picked up by the steamer *Scindia* and landed here.

On the following day the news suggested that the *Jeddah* did not founder as reported by the master and had arrived in Aden, with all the pilgrims on board, in tow of the steamer *Antenor*.

Aden: August 11, 1880

The *Jeddah* which was abandoned at sea with 953 pilgrims on board, did not founder, as reported by the master. She has just arrived here, all safe, in tow of the steamer *Antenor*.

With the publication of leading articles in the newspapers of Singapore and England, this story of cowardice at sea and how the captain and crew of the *Jeddah* had abandoned the long-held principle that they should be the last to leave a sinking ship, kept Singapore buzzing. Maritime Court inquiries were held in both Aden and Singapore and official sanctions made. This story would have been a continuing subject of discussion wherever sailors met in Singapore and there is no doubt that it was here, after his arrival from the ship *Palestine* in 1881, that Joseph Conrad first heard the story which would later become the basis of his novel *Lord Jim*.

6

Voyage of the *Jeddah*, 1880

The whole waterside talked of nothing else – every confounded
loafer in the town came in for a harvest of drinks over this affair
... you heard it in the Harbour Office, you heard it at every
shipbrokers, at your agents, from whites, natives, from half
castes, from the very boatmen squatting half-naked on the stone
steps as you went up from the Landing-Stage.

Joseph Conrad, *Lord Jim*

The 993-ton steamship *Jeddah* left Singapore in July 1880 for
Penang to pick up Muslim pilgrims bound for the Holy Land. The
ship was owned by Syed Mohsin bin Salleh Al Joffree who was
listed in the Singapore Register as a merchant and ship owner of
36 Raffles Place and his son Seyyid Omar was on board. There
were seven European officers including Captain Clark, the first
mate Austin Williams, who became the Lord Jim of Conrad's
story, the second mate, as well as the chief, second and third
engineers.

The official complement of the steamer upon leaving Penang

was given as 992 pilgrims who were cramped together, with little room to move and very little fresh air unless they travelled deck passage and were then exposed to the blazing heat of the equatorial sun. The 778 men, 147 women, and 67 children were sustained only by the meagre food they had brought with them for the three-week voyage to the port of Jeddah. The passengers were making this pilgrimage to Mecca to fulfil one of the five central commandments of the Muslim faith, as every Muslim, if they have the means to do so, should perform this pilgrimage at least once in their life. Many had invested their life savings, as well as that of their family, in making this journey. Some might not return to their native villages, but to return was not essential, as to die on the pilgrimage is seen as a blessing. Joseph Conrad describes the loading of the pilgrims in *Lord Jim*:

> They streamed aboard over three gangways , they streamed in urged by faith and the hope of paradise, they streamed in with a continuous tramp and shuffle of bare feet, without a word, a murmur, or a look back; and when clear of confining rails spread on all sides over the deck, flowed forward and aft, overflowed down the yawning hatchways, filled the inner recesses of the ship – like water filling a cistern, like water flowing into crevices and crannies, like water rising silently even with the rim ... They had collected there, coming from the north and south and from the outskirts of the East, after treading the jungle paths, descending the rivers, coasting in praus along the shallows, crossing in small canoes from island

to island, passing through suffering, meeting strange sights, beset by strange fears, upheld by one desire.

The well-to-do had made shelters with heavy boxes and dusty mats, the poor reposed side by side with all they had on earth tied up in a rag under their heads, the lone old men slept with drawn-up legs upon their prayer-carpets. A father, his shoulders up and his knees under his forehead, dozed by a boy who slept on his back, a woman covered from head to foot, like a corpse, with a piece of white sheeting, had a naked child in the hollow of each arm.

As it steamed ahead the *Jeddah* left behind the white streak of its wake on a calm equatorial sea, and Austin Williams was grateful for this peace of sea and sky as he plotted the vessel's course across the Indian Ocean and towards the entrance to the Red Sea. The passage towards the Holy Place, towards Mecca, towards the promise of salvation and the reward of eternal life.

On 3 August 1880, while off the coast of the Horn of Africa and in gale-force winds and heavy seas, the ship's boilers drifted from their mountings and the crew used wedges to reseat them. On 6 August the weather worsened and the wedges holding the boilers in place began to give way. Leaks developed and the ship stopped to make repairs. Thereafter the *Jeddah* proceeded slowly with only one boiler lit. However, the leaks increased and despite the efforts of the crew and passengers trying to bail out the water, she began to take on more water due to leaks in the supply lines. The *Jeddah* again stopped for repairs, during which time and as she rolled in the heavy seas, her boilers broke loose, and all connection pipes were washed away, rendering her engines ineffective.

The derelict and waterlogged *Jeddah* could not be steered and was now drifting helplessly towards Cape Guardafui at the entrance to the Red Sea. The ship was in danger of sinking and all the traditions and training of the merchant marine taught the captain and his crew that it was their responsibility to help save the passengers, even above that of saving their own lives. However, their vessel was inadequately equipped with lifeboats. They could do the arithmetic – there was room for only one quarter of the passengers to crowd into the lifeboats. They could each imagine the mayhem and chaos that would ensue as 992 pilgrims tried to board only seven lifeboats.

At 2 am and under cover of darkness, Captain Clark and his British officers were preparing to launch the lifeboats. Upon discovering this, the pilgrims, who until then had been helping to bail out water from the engine room, tried to prevent the crew from abandoning them. A fight ensued, resulting in some of the crew falling overboard and drowning. As the captain, his wife and the chief engineer sat in the first lifeboat, the passengers threw whatever they could onto the boat to prevent it from being lowered. They struggled with the first mate, who was lowering the boat from the ship, causing him to fall overboard. The lifeboat was eventually lowered and the first mate was pulled from the sea into the lifeboat. Thus, the captain, his wife, the chief engineer, the first officer and several other crew members escaped in one of the lifeboats, taking the shipowner's son Seyyid Omar with them and leaving the pilgrims and the remaining officers and crew on board the *Jeddah*. After the captain's lifeboat had been launched, the second mate tried to lower another lifeboat along with a few passengers. However, other passengers tried to prevent this, and in the confusion that ensued, the lifeboat fell into the water, drowning the second mate and the pilgrims on board.

As the captain's lifeboat headed for the sea-lane where they expected to encounter Suez Canal shipping, they concocted a story of how they remained near the ship until they had seen her sink. The story needed to include ramming a floating object:

Shock slight. Stopped the ship. Ascertained the damage. Took measures to get the boats out without creating a panic. As the first boat was lowered, ship went down in a squall. Sank like lead.

At 10 am and fewer than seven hours after abandoning their ship the lifeboat was sighted by the Liverpool steamship *Scindia*, bound for Port Said. All twenty-one in the lifeboat including Captain Clark, his wife, and the chief mate, Williams, were safely taken aboard. Importantly Captain Clark made no request for a search to be made for the *Jeddah* or any pilgrims that might have survived its probable sinking.

However, the *Jeddah* had not sunk. The remaining crew members, with the help of the pilgrims, continued bailing the water out of the ship's engine room. They hoisted distress signals which were sighted by the British steamship *Antenor* only six hours after Captain Clark had been taken safely aboard the *Scindia*. The *Antenor*'s first mate, Randolph Campbell, boarded the *Jeddah* and believed the derelict ship might be towed to Aden if they could manage to keep her afloat. With patience, skill and ingenuity, the *Jeddah* was then safely towed into Aden without any loss of life and Campbell later described to the Court of Inquiry:

> I called the headmen amongst the pilgrims together and organised gangs amongst them to pump and bale the vessel. This was done, the men constantly relieving each one another, and by the evening of the 9th of August, we had gained 6 inches on the water, and during the following night we gained a foot on the water and continued to gain on the water thenceforward until the water was reduced to 3 ½ feet in the engine room and 5 feet in the after hold.

The news announcing the supposed loss of the steamer *Jeddah* with one thousand souls on board created a huge sensation and thrill of horror when first published in London. To be replaced by a completely different feeling when the news was received that the steamer had been towed safely into Aden with all her hapless passengers, and that she had been abandoned, prematurely, by the captain and his officers. For the *Times* it was the subject of an indignant editorial on August 12, 1880:

> Nothing can be more admirable than the manner in which, as a rule, the commanders of vessels in distress stay by them to the end, and insist on being the last rather than the first to be saved … It would have been terrible

that more than nine hundred helpless pilgrims should have perished at sea. But that they should have been abandoned by the officers of the ship to which they had entrusted themselves, and saved by the accidental services rendered them by another vessel, is scarcely credible.

A court of inquiry was held at Aden and Captain Clark's statement to the court read:

At noon on the second August there was a moderate gale and rising sea, causing the engines to race and the vessel to pitch badly and shipping much water forward ... at seven pm the foretopmast sail was blown away, and the water from the broken closet pipes continued to come into the fore and aft cabins, so the leaks could not be got at. During the third August the wind blew a very strong gale and a fearful sea was running, washing the decks clear fore and aft of two native water closets and all moveables, and causing a heavy strain on the engines and boilers.

The wind increased to hurricane force and the high seas crashing over the vessel's decks and the rolling of the ship in mountainous seas put a great a strain on the vessel, the jerking of the boilers broke the connecting pipes and the *Jeddah* was shipping vast quantities of water. Of the final day of chaos on board, Captain Clark gave a graphic picture:

At 7 am on the seventh of August, it was still blowing

a tremendous gale, and the water in the vessel rose above the fire grates, the boilers started adrift from their seatings, and the stoke hole and engine-room plates and bearers dashed about with every roll of the vessel. It now seemed that the vessel had sprung a heavy leak probably caused by the boilers knocking a hole in the ship's side, and as nothing more could be done in the engine room and the water was rising so rapidly, every deck pump was set to work and the firemen and passengers employed day and night at the pumps and bailing water with buckets.

At midnight on the seventh to eighth the passengers refused to pump any more, and the vessel settled down by the stern with a heavy list to starboard, and at 2 am this appearer left the vessel in one of the ship's boats and arrived in Aden on the tenth of August.

Captain Clark had ordered the ship's lifeboats to be prepared and swung out early that morning, an act which caused considerable panic amongst the pilgrims as there was room for no more than a quarter of the passengers to crowd into the lifeboats. And in fact, it was under the cover of the darkness of night that the Captain and his officers abandoned the ship.

The first mate of the *Jeddah,* Austin Williams, according to his own statement to the court, advised the captain to leave the ship, telling him his life was in danger, also his wife's life; that he, the master was sure to be killed if he remained on board; and that he, the first mate, did thrust the master into the boat. The mate worked on the fears of the master for the safety of his wife, and by so doing hurried the master into leaving the ship.

The court of inquiry in Aden considered that with 992 passengers on board a vessel of the tonnage of the *Jeddah* that it was seriously overloaded. The court criticised *Jeddah*'s chief engineer for incorrect operation of the boilers. It found the actions of Captain Clark in swinging out *Jeddah*'s lifeboats prematurely and subsequently launching the boats, and thus causing panic amongst the passengers to be unprofessional conduct and that he showed a want of judgement. The court concluded that Captain Clark was guilty of gross misconduct in being indirectly the cause of the deaths of the second mate, seven crew, and ten passengers, and in abandoning his disabled ship with nearly one thousand souls on board to their fate. The court also remarked on the want of anxiety shown by the master for the fate of the *Jeddah* by not doing all in his power to induce the Master of the *Scindia* to search for possible survivors. The court of inquiry also commended the actions of the master and first mate of *Antenor* for its rescue of the *Jeddah*.

The courage which failed him on board the *Jeddah* supported Austin Williams through two withering courtroom investigations where the condemnation he seemed to seek was readily given. William's compulsion to volunteer a self-damaging statement to the court led to the session judge describing it as:

> The most extraordinary instance known to the Court of the abandonment of a disabled and leaking ship at sea by the master and Europeans, and almost all the crew, with close on 1000 souls on board when no immediate danger

existed of her foundering.

In conclusion, the court ordered that Joseph Lucas Clark's certificate of competency as master be suspended for a period of three years. In regard to the first mate, one of the two judges at the Aden hearing stated in his appended verdict that the first mate of the *Jeddah*, according to his own statement, was greatly to blame in doing what he could to demoralise the master, by advising him to leave the ship, telling him his life was in danger, also his wife's life, that he, the master, was sure to be killed if he remained on board, and that he the first mate did thrust the master into the boat. However, Austin Williams received only a reprimand:

The Court consider it necessary to place on record their disapprobation of the conduct of the first officer of the Jeddah, Mr Williams, who may be said to have more than aided and abetted the master in the abandonment of his vessel ... But for Mr. William's officious behaviour and unseaman-like conduct, the master would have probably done his duty by remaining on the ship.

A second inquiry into the abandonment of the *Jeddah* was held in Singapore and it reported that the facts seemed very simple. That the ship being, in the opinion of the captain, in danger of sinking, he proceeded to get out the boats, not with the intention of caring for the lives of those who had to look to him, and to no one else, for their protection under these circumstances – whom he was bound as much by duty as by feelings of common humanity to make his first consideration, – but simply to provide for his wife – which might be natural enough, if he had remembered that other people on board his sinking ship had wives as well as himself. The report concluded that not only did he disgracefully desert the ship and passengers, but next morning, when one would think he had had time to reflect, he apparently gave not one thought to these poor creatures whom he had so cruelly deserted, nor does he suggest to the captain of the *Scindia* that they should put about and search for survivors who could be floating upon some fragment of wreck, but went contentedly on to Aden.

The Vice-Admiralty Court in Singapore, meeting in September 1881 to consider the amount of salvage to be paid, found that the pilgrims became agitated only when they realised that they were being left to die by the crew. They had not threatened violence as had been alleged in defence of the decision to abandon them. Indeed, the judgment says, they did not use their knives to injure anyone. The master had communicated nothing to them, and their 'demeanour' could be quite reasonably accounted for by the realisation that they were being deserted: the master's leaving the ship 'roused the pilgrims to violence in attempting to swamp his boat, and such the Court consider might naturally have been expected from any body of human beings, even Europeans, situated as the pilgrims were.'

Kept alive by harbour talk, the *Jeddah* story grew into a sailors' legend, bolstered by court proceedings, newspaper accounts, endless waterfront debate and the presence of Austin Williams among the seamen working in the harbour of Singapore. Even seventy years later, in 1950, *The Straits Times* recalled how this cowardly disregard of the traditions of the sea had caused such a tremendous sensation in Singapore. Despite the two official inquiries, Austin Williams was never brought to trial. He might have returned to anonymity in England and to face his parson father there, which would have been a brave action in its way, but he was adamant. 'No, my dad will have seen it in all the home papers by this time. He would never understand.' Branded a coward in full sight and in full hearing of the world, he continued to live in Singapore and work in its harbour and amongst its seamen for the next thirty-four years as a water-clerk. Such a job meant racing under sail, steam or oars against other water-clerks for any ship about to anchor, greeting her captain cheeringly, forcing upon him the business card of a ship chandler and on his first visit on shore piloting him to the firm's shop. A job requiring ability, agility, stamina and a certain amount of presence and guile. Williams was a brave man – of a certain kind. After what had happened, he would have had to be brave to take a job with a ship chandler located right next door to where sailors often met at Emmerson's Tiffin Rooms.

It is not known if Joseph Conrad ever met Austin Williams in Singapore. But by the time he came to write *Lord Jim* he certainly knew that Williams worked as a water-clerk in that port, and they could easily have passed on the landing steps of Johnstone Pier, in a ship chandler's office or on the street outside Emmerson's.

7

East Borneo

The seventeenth-century traders went there for pepper,
because the passion for pepper seemed to burn like a flame
of love in the breast of Dutch and English adventurers about the
time of James the First. Where wouldn't they go for pepper!
For a bag of pepper they would cut each other's throats
without hesitation ... the bizarre obstinacy of that desire
made them defy death in a thousand shapes; the unknown
seas, the loathsome and strange diseases; wounds,
captivity, hunger, pestilence and despair.
Joseph Conrad, *Lord Jim*

From Singapore, Konrad Korzeniowski's next destination would be Borneo. Borneo! I can still remember how the name alone would fire my own boyhood imagination. I would envisage a world of Malay Sultans and White Rajahs, fierce pirates and beautiful princesses. Wild rivers and steamy jungles filled with tattooed headhunters armed with poison blowpipes. Its jungles the last sanctuary of wild animals like the orang-hutan – 'the wild man of Borneo'– the clouded leopard, the hornbill and of strange, rarely visited Dyak tribes living in the remote mountains of the interior.

The Europeans – Portuguese, Spanish, Dutch and English – travelled to the East Indies in search of exotic spices such as pepper, cloves and nutmeg from the early sixteenth century. But it was the Dutch who prevailed, and the Dutch East India Company established by force of arms their monopoly over the spice trade in cloves and nutmeg from the Moluccas (Maluku) in the eastern archipelago. Both the Dutch and the English traded for pepper at Banten in West Java and at Palembang in South Sumatra, but eventually these ports were controlled by the Dutch East India Company, so the English East India Company was forced to trade in the more remote ports of the archipelago such as Bencoolen in West Sumatra and Banjarmasin in South Borneo.

In the European imagination, the island of Borneo, the third largest island in the world, located on the equator and situated in the geographical centre of the Malay-Indonesian archipelago, has always been associated with danger, mystery and excitement. These very real dangers included Dyak headhunters, who populated the interior, snakes, crocodiles and malarial mosquitos that filled its swamps and jungles, and Illanun pirates who raided ships and Borneo's coastal villages.

Two hundred years ago piracy was rampant in the Malay-Indonesian archipelago, particularly off the coast of Borneo. From Manila to Sumatra, from Malacca to the Celebes, no merchant ship or coastal village was safe from pirates. In those days the archipelago was divided into countless petty kingdoms and each rajah or sultan seemed to be the commander-in-chief of a pirate fleet. These squadrons could shelter in a thousand isolated bays, a thousand rivers and a thousand coastal swamps which offered hiding places from where they could launch raids. Lightly armed trading vessels stood little chance against these ruthless warriors who came sweeping across the seas, brandishing their two-handed swords, and yelling war cries as they leapt on deck in quest of plunder and slaves.

Illanun pirates roamed the Sulu Sea and the coast of Borneo from their homeland on the island of Mindanao in the southern Philippines. They were the fiercest and most powerful pirates of the Eastern Seas. They might give quarter to a native crew, being fellow Muslims, but for any white men they showed no mercy. Their warships were built sharp in the prow and wide in the beam, could exceed ninety feet in length and could carry as many as one hundred rowers and warriors. In place of a fixed mast these boats were fitted with a swivel which allowed the mast to be raised or lowered very swiftly and upon it was hoisted a huge woven rattan sail. Installed in the bow was a long gun, in the stern was a brass cannon and along its sides were various swivel guns. Each man was a rower as well as a warrior equipped with a spear, a short kris and an Illanun sword, whose handle was long enough to be wielded with two hands and was designed to separate a head from its body in a single blow. Piracy had become a hereditary career for Illanun people. Their fathers and the fathers of their fathers had done the same and like those who closely embrace death they were fearless, 'We strike and go, we live and die with our weapons in our hands.' Their objective was plunder and slaves. The plunder was found in the ships they boarded and the slaves in the coastal villages they attacked. Slaves were more lucrative than loot as there was always a ready market for young men to perform manual labour and for young women to serve as concubines, who if they were particularly good-looking were saved for the Batavia market and it was only in 1863 that the Dutch banned slavery in the East Indies.

James Brooke sailed for western Borneo in his private yacht *Royalist*, arriving in Kuching in 1839. Three years later he received a grant of the territory of Sarawak from the Sultan of Brunei, which enabled him to rule in his own right as the 'White Rajah' of Sarawak in return for an annual payment. With the support of the British China Squadron, he embarked on a campaign against piracy on the west coast of Borneo, comprising first the Iban people of the Saribas and Skrang rivers north of Sarawak, then raiders from Marudu Bay, as well as the Illanun raiders under the suzerainty of the Sultanate of Sulu. The Illanun pirates were also active down the coast of East Borneo, raiding coastal villages and capturing trading vessels. At this time the Dutch only had a single naval frigate based in Macassar to control the whole Straits of Macassar, and the coastal villages felt they were given little protection by the Dutch. The following account from the *Semarang Courant* of January 1876 describes a complaint from William Lingard to the Dutch authorities:

> Mr. Lingard commander of the *West Indian*, which vessel we stated at length last week had been attacked by pirates off the east coast of Borneo has again treated of the event in the *Macassar Handelsblad*. He is of the opinion that

the honour of the Dutch flag is very badly maintained on the east coast of Borneo and it is high time to guard the coast more effectively.

The rivers of East Borneo, such as the Kapuas, Seruyan, Barito, Mahakam, Berau, Kayan and Sesayap, were the geographic highways that provided the only means to transport people and goods through the dense forests and mountains of Borneo and provide a connection between the coastal Malays and the Dyaks of the interior.

At the mouth of the Barito River on the south coast of Borneo lay the settlement of Banjarmasin and it was here that the English East India Company ship *Eagle Galley* arrived in 1714. Captain Daniel Beekmans' mission was to reopen the pepper trade with the Sultanate of Banjarmasin after a conflict a few years before had resulted in the execution of those English traders who were unable to escape. His report describes the products found in Banjarmasin:

The Country abounds with pepper, the best dragons-blood resin, most excellent camphor and all sorts of fruit that are generally found in any part of the East Indies. The mountains yield diamonds, gold, tin, and iron: the forests yield honey, cotton, deer, goats, buffalo, wild oxen, wild hogs, small horses, bears, tigers, elephants and a multitude of monkeys.

Dragon's blood resin is produced from a certain type of rattan palm. It is gathered by breaking off the layer of red resin encasing the unripe fruit of the rattan. The collected resin is then rolled into solid balls before being sold for use as a varnish, incense and dye. Beekman clearly understood why the sultan and his people wanted to keep the English East India Company from getting too close to the source of their wealth:

> The Dyaks come down the river to the port of Banjar Masseen in very ill-shaped praus; and bring down gold-dust, diamonds, bezoar-stones, rattans and sundry other merchandise. The Banjareens will not suffer the Europeans to have any acquaintance or trade with them, but do purchase the goods from them, which they sell to us at a greater price. I do verily believe that the many frightful stories they tell of these people's barbarity and cruelty, are only invented on purpose to deter us from having any acquaintance or commerce with them.

Rattan is a climbing vine of various sizes according to how long it has grown before harvest. It furnished the material for the manufacture of an endless variety of useful objects throughout the region including furniture. There was a saying that: 'Take away bamboo and you take away a Malay house, take away rattan and you take away the furniture.' Rattan provided sleeping mats, sitting mats, boxes and baskets of all shapes and sizes, besides threads, cords and ropes.

The settlement of Banjarmasin was of strategic importance because of its position at the mouth of the Barito River and as a major port on the Java Sea. British merchant explorer Alexander Hare arrived in Banjarmasin after the British East India Company seized Java from Dutch control in 1811. Stamford Raffles had met Hare in Malacca where he ran trading voyages between Malacca, Penang and Borneo and Raffles appointed Hare the Resident at Banjarmasin. Hare managed to acquire a land grant of 1,400 square miles from the Sultan of Banjarmasin and established it as an independent state and a personal fiefdom which he named Maluka. Raffles reasoned that if Hare could establish himself as a sultan in his own right, like James Brooke, then there would be no legal argument for giving this territory back to the Dutch when peace came to Europe. Hare needed people to work his pepper plantations and Raffles decreed that petty criminals should be sent as indentured labourers to Banjarmasin and assigned to Hare, who even received a subsidy for every criminal he took. However, the pepper failed to flourish and Hare became infamous for establishing a harem and trading his slaves. Consequently, when the Dutch returned to the East Indies after 1815, Hare was forced to leave Banjarmasin and his failed colony of Maluka (together with his harem). Hare eventually settled on a deserted island atoll in the Indian Ocean southeast of Java, and descendants of intermarriage between ladies from his harem and passing sailors, many of them Scottish, are the present-day Cocos-Keeling islanders, who wear Malay dress and perform traditional Scottish reels.

After the return of the Dutch, they appointed a Resident in Banjarmasin and effective power in the sultanate was increasingly taken over by the Dutch. The Dutch were mainly interested in the pepper trade but the port was the outlet for all the natural forest products which came down the river as well as gold, tin and diamonds. In 1837, coal was also discovered in the interior thus the Dutch took an interest in coal mines, increasing Banjarmasin's economic and strategic importance. The Dutch managed to involve themselves in a quarrel over the choice of a new sultan by providing military support to the candidate of their choice and when he did become sultan he served as their vassal. The main problem was that, according to traditional law, the new puppet sultan was never recognised as legitimate. During a people's revolt in 1859, Dutch troops were required to put down the rebellion and the struggle caused considerable loss of life and immense damage to property in parts of southern Borneo. By 1862, Dutch troops had won the upper hand, the sultanate was disbanded and the Dutch gained direct control. As part of their war booty the Dutch seized the 'Banjarmasin Diamond'. Once owned by the Sultan of Banjarmasin, the stone was a state heirloom and a symbol of the sultan's sovereignty. After the sultanate was abolished, the rough diamond was sent to the Netherlands, where it was cut into a multifaceted rectangle of forty carats and is displayed to this day in the Rijksmuseum.

The major river system in East Borneo is the Mahakam and its tributaries, which drain a huge area. The Kutei people live along the Mahakam River and the eastern coast of Borneo. The Kutei kingdom was the oldest Hindu kingdom in Indonesia, as evidenced by the discovery there of four stone stupa from AD 400 engraved in Pallawa script. As Islam spread through the Indonesian archipelago in the 14th and 15th centuries it gradually supplanted Hinduism. The Sultan of Kutei ruled from his palace at Tenggarong which is eighty miles up the Mahakam River. The palace is now the Mulawarman Museum, which houses the Kutai Martadipura and Kutai Kartanegara royal treasures. During the long struggle for control of Macassar, many Bugis fled their motherland to eastern Borneo and the Sultan of Kutei allowed them to settle downstream from Tenggarong in what became the city of Samarinda. Here they were subject to their own leaders and were semi-independent from the Sultan of Kutei. Political power in East Borneo and along the mighty Mahakam River and its tributaries may have been in the hands of the Sultan of Kutei, but his authority did not extend far into the Dyak territories of the interior or far into the Bugis settlement at Samarinda.

In 1825, the Dutch government in Batavia sent Major George Muller with a small military escort to Tenggarong to negotiate a treaty with the Sultan of Kutei and to explore the interior of Borneo. After the signing of the treaty his party set off to explore the lands further upstream. His mission was to explore the upper reaches of the Mahakam and if possible to cross over the watershed into the Kapuas basin and travel downstream to Pontianak. However, it appears they were attacked and killed by Dyak headhunters near what are now called the Muller Mountains. The exact circumstances of their deaths are unknown as the region remained terra incognita for some time. It would appear that the Muller expedition did cross over into the Kapuas basin and many believe he was killed by order of the Sultan of Kutei, but since the murder had occurred in the Kapuas drainage, the sultan could not, of course, be held accountable.

Almost forty years later, in 1844 the Scottish adventurer James Erskine Murray, fourth son of the Earl of Elibank, reached the mouth of the Mahakam River with two heavily manned vessels bristling with arms. They were the schooner *Young Queen* which carried an 18-pound pivot-gun amidships, a 12-pound pivot-gun on the forecastle, two 4-pound stern chasers as well as six small pivot-guns on the broadsides, and the brig *Anna* carrying four 4-pounders on either broadside as well as a pivot-gun on the top gallant forecastle. Rifles, pistols, cutlasses and boarding-pikes completed the armaments. The fleet found its way through the multitude of channels that formed the delta and then made its way upstream. When they reached the settlement of Samarinda, Murray anchored and fired off a gun salute. The crew were surprised when there was a salute in return from an onshore battery with guns that appeared of equal calibre to their own. They were even more surprised to learn that the settlement was not occupied by the Borneo Dyaks or the coastal Malays, but by the Bugis of Sulawesi who were highly regarded for their bravery and fighting skills. At a meeting with the Bugis leaders, Murray was told that if he wanted to trade in Samarinda he must first obtain permission from the Sultan of Kutei at Tenggarong, another forty miles upriver.

Although Murray insisted he had come to trade, nobody from Singapore to Shanghai doubted that he had ambitions to be another James Brooke, a White Rajah, and that his real goal was conquest and settlement. Further upriver Murray was able to meet with the Sultan of Kutei and propose terms of trade, including requesting land to build a trading post and for the exclusive right to run steamships up the river. He was told the sultan was favourable but would need to consult with his chiefs as was the Malay practice. This was a delaying tactic, and Murray later observed activity to strengthen the gun batteries onshore as well as local boats carrying large numbers of armed men downstream which could obstruct the withdrawal of his expedition. The sultan then returned Murray's trade goods insisting that trade on the river was controlled by the Bugis located downstream in Samarinda and that to trade in Kutei he must either deal with, or destroy, the Bugis of Samarinda. Murray recorded that during his time in Tenggarong 'he had tried by all possible means to gain the friendship of the people so that a vast field for British enterprise and manufacturing might be opened up in this part of Borneo.' He came to the conclusion that the Bugis had gained control over the sultan and his subjects and monopolised the trade on the river. By opening foreign trade directly with the sultan and the Dyak people, Murray thought they would be glad to be freed of their Bugis oppressors, but according to him the sultan proved to be 'a bad man whose life was one continued course of murder and piracy.'

An attempt was then made to board Murray's ship and this was followed by a firefight. It was obviously time to leave and as they made their way downstream the two vessels were pursued by some fifty war-boats which put them under continuous fire from their muskets, and lower downstream hidden batteries opened fire with cannon. This running battle continued all day and the fleet feared what would happen when they reached Samarinda. Fortunately, this happened after dark and even though the Bugis had lit fires on the opposite bank of the river to better see

Murray's ships in profile, their cannon could not get good range and caused little damage. On reaching the delta, the *Young Queen* and the *Anna* were forced to wait for the incoming tide and with it sufficient water to allow them to navigate through its channels. As they lay helpless in the delta they again came under attack and James Erskine Murray and two of his crew were killed by gunfire before their vessels were able to escape to the open waters of the Macassar Strait.

The voyage to Kutei of James Erskine Murray caused the Dutch to pay a lot more attention to East Borneo and they sent a naval mission to Tenggarong to establish a treaty with the Sultan of Kutei. It is probably no surprise that he agreed to surrender his sovereignty to the Dutch as the agreement established a Dutch Resident in Samarinda and allowed him to seize the lucrative position of harbourmaster there from the Buginese. This was important because the sultan did not have a large population of Malay supporters compared to the Dyak and Bugis populations and his rule was based on the patronage he distributed from the taxes and royalties he could collect. Dutch rule was established with the arrival in 1846 of H. von Dewall, the first civil administrator on the east coast of Borneo.

Carl Bock, a Norwegian naturalist, was commissioned by the Dutch Colonial authorities to make another journey of exploration into the little explored districts of East Borneo in 1879. He was required to report on the natives of the interior of the Sultanate of Kutei and to collect flora and fauna. His plan was to travel up the Mahakam River, then up one of its tributaries before crossing the watershed to the Barito River, and travelling all the way downstream to Banjarmasin. His journey was the first of its kind since George Muller's ill-fated expedition of twenty-five years earlier and would open up new unexplored territory for the Dutch. In his book *The Head-Hunters of Borneo*, Bock describes the trade from Samarinda:

> At the time of my arrival there were five vessels – three of them barques of considerable size – all belonging to Chinamen, being loaded with the produce of the country, which is brought down the river on long rafts. Rattan is the staple product; but also gutta-percha (native rubber), timber, beeswax, damar and edible birds' nests. The imports are rice, salt, opium, gambier, coffee, petroleum, coloured prints, white and black calico, iron, brass wire, cocoa-nuts and cocoa-nut oil.

Bock had an introduction to the Sultan of Kutei, who met him at his palace in Tenggarong, a building which impressed Bock no more than did the sultan himself whom he describes as:

> A clean shaven, fleshy, and rather heavy-looking face was set off by a pair of extraordinarily bright eyes, flashing like fire. The lips were parted by a pleasant smile as he advanced to greet me and revealed a set of teeth as black as Whitby jet from betel chewing.

Bock was warned of the threat of Dyak headhunters, and the Sultan of Kutei offered some of his staff as guides. Bock's party made an initial foray up the Mahakam River to Muara Kaman and then northwards up the Telen River into Dyak territory. It was at Muara Kaman that Bock describes being secretly attacked by hosts of bloodthirsty enemies who stole upon them in the night – these enemies taking the form neither of Dyak headhunters nor Malay bandits, but myriads of mosquitoes. Bock wrote how people would laugh to think that the expedition had been turned back not by head-hunting Dyaks but by bloodthirsty mosquitoes.

On returning to Tenggarong, Bock was present at the celebrations marking the sultan's forty-third birthday. The bill of fare included soup and the sultan's favourite dish of beefsteak and asparagus, all washed down with Champagne. This was followed by Malay and Dyak dances and then the appearance of the sultan in his formal dress:

> Suddenly there was a general hush as the Sultan was seen to enter the audience-chamber again and take his seat on the throne. This time he was dressed in a Governor-General's uniform, and wore on his head the massive gold crown, weighing something like four pounds, and in a shape not unlike the Papal mitre. Suspended around his neck glistened a huge diamond, as large as a pigeon's egg.

The Bock expedition made its way upstream to the Upper Mahakam and then to Muara Anang on the left-hand branch of the Upper Mahakam. Bock then reached the territory of the Tring Dyaks who were to guide him over the mountainous watershed to the Barito River. For this journey Bock was accompanied by no less than fifty-two Dyak coolies and an armed escort of twenty-two Bugis mercenaries provided by the sultan to ensure his safety. From here they made a four-day overland trek to Muara Benangan on a branch of the Barito River. This was the most arduous and dangerous part of Bock's journey, to cross the watershed a path had to be cut through the deep jungle and the expedition had to negotiate narrow bamboo bridges across rivers. From here the expedition travelled down the Barito River and reached Banjarmasin.

The Berau River is one of five large rivers on the east coast of Borneo that straddle the equator and drain into the Sulawesi Sea. Tanjong Redeb, with its small Malay settlement forty miles up the river, is described by Conrad as 'One of the lost, forgotten, unknown places of the earth.' The sultanates of Gunung Tabour and Sambaliung were created by Malay traders who imposed their authority over the Dyaks of the interior in the early 1800s. In 1844 Captain Belcher of HMS *Samarang* had cause to visit Gunung Tabour, which is opposite Tanjung Redeb, when he received a message for help from the crew of the British vessel *Premier* which had struck a reef off the coast near the Berau River and claimed to be held captive by the sultan. On his arrival in Gunung Tabour, Captain Belcher was cordially received by the sultan and escorted to the royal audience hall where he learned that the seven British members of the crew had been taken away by a Dutch schooner-of-war some months earlier. He also learned that the Dutch had not yet annexed this part of Borneo and that the sultan had no agreement with any other nation. With no effective Dutch control in the region they concluded the following agreement:

The Sultan of Gunung Tabour is anxious to enter into friendly relations with Her Majesty the Queen of Great Britain, and is willing to enter into a formal Treaty of Friendship and Commerce whenever Her Majesty the Queen of Great Britain will send any authorised person.

The Sultan of Gunung Tabour engages, that the subjects of the Queen of Great Britain shall always meet with friendship and protection within his dominions.

On the part of the Queen of Great Britain, Sir Edward Belcher, commanding *HMS Samarang*, engages, that similar friendship and protection will be accorded to the subjects of the Sultan of Gunung Tabour, should they visit any of the ports belonging to Great Britain.

Frank Marryat, who accompanied Captain Belcher, describes in detail the Dyaks they met at Gunung Tabour:

We fell in with a most remarkable tribe of Dyaks, they wore immense rings in their ears of tin or copper, the weight of which extended their ears to an extraordinary extent. On their heads they wore a mass of feathers of argus pheasant, they wore on their shoulders skins of leopards and wild cats and necklaces of beads and teeth. They were armed with the usual parang, blowpipe and shield. The standard exchange from them was gold and a small bamboo of gold was worth the equivalent of twenty Dutch guilders in trade goods.

It was around 1878 that this part of East Borneo was made a Dutch protectorate, and a Dutch Resident was appointed. One of the first acts of Jacobus Jozephus Meijer was to persuade the sultans of Gunung Tabour and Sambaliung to sign an agreement whereby the kidnapping and export of slaves was forbidden, that no torturing or mutilating of criminals would be allowed, that no punishment with death or banishment would be allowed without the sanction of the Dutch Resident, that the sultans would fight pirates found on the sea, beaches or river, that all ships in distress along the coast or on the river would be given assistance.

Sailing down the coast of East Borneo, William Lingard heard that a new Malay settlement had been established at Gunung Tabour on the Berau River. He then surveyed the numerous channels that formed the delta at the entrance to that river and after discovering what became known as Lingard's Crossing – Oversteek van Lingard on Dutch charts – he reached the settlement. As described by the Eastern Archipelago Pilot:

> The approach to the Berau river is an extensive estuary, formed by many uninhabited islands, with various passages between them … the channels through the estuary are only suitable for small vessels with local knowledge … The principle channel of approach leads through … the upper reaches of the Muara Garura … There are also navigable approaches through Muara Pantai, on the southern side of the estuary, and Muara Tidong on the north side … Muara Pantai is now seldom used.

Lingard was able to take his brig forty miles upstream to the settlement. It was here that he reached an agreement with the sultan to establish a trading station and he extended his own authority to an extent almost comparable to that of James Brooke, the 'White Rajah' of Sarawak. However, unlike Brooke his main interest was in trade rather than the establishment of territorial rule. The principal articles of export from the Berau River were rattan, damar (gum resin) and gutta-percha from a tree which oozed a rubbery, workable and waterproof substance. No doubt his motivation at the time was personal gain but he soon established good relations with the ruler and the people, and with the permission of the Sultan he was granted a monopoly over the export of forest products from the years 1860 to 1870.

It was in 1887 that Konrad Korzeniowski made his first voyage to East Borneo, to the Berau River, and to the settlements of Gunung Tabour and Tanjung Redeb as the first mate on the trading ship *Vidar* and to the trading post that William Lingard had established there. This was important for his writing life because the river and the settlement provided the location and the characters which he would reimagine in his novels.

8

Voyages of the *Vidar*, 1887-1888

She was an Eastern ship, inasmuch as then she belonged to
those seas. She traded among dark islands on a blue reef-scarred
sea, with the Red Ensign over the taffrail and at her masthead
a house-flag, also red, but with a green border and with a
white crescent in it. For an Arab owned her, and a Syed at that.
Hence the green border on the flag.

Joseph Conrad, *The Shadow-Line*

Between voyages, sailors would spend days, weeks or even
months in a foreign port. In Singapore, the main seamen's lodging
was Sailors' Home, which was established in the 1850s on High
Street but which by 1892 had moved to a two-storey house on
the corner of North Bridge Road and Stamford Road, the site
of the present-day Capitol Building. While waiting for their next
berth, men spent their time swapping stories with fellow seafarers
in Sailors' Home and in the bars and eating houses in the port
area. Joseph Conrad describes the two kinds of sailing men he

met in Singapore. The majority were men who were thrown there by some accident and had remained in Singapore as officers of local ships. They now had a horror of long voyages with their harder conditions, severer view of duty and the hazards of stormy oceans. As described by Conrad in *Lord Jim*, these men were now attuned to the eternal peace of the Eastern seas:

> They loved short passages, good deckchairs, large native crews, and the distinction of being white. They shuddered at the thought of hard work, and led precariously easy lives, always on the verge of dismissal, always on the verge of engagement, serving Chinamen, Arabs, half-castes and would have served the devil himself had he made it easy enough. They talked everlastingly of turns of luck: how So-and-so got charge of a boat on the coast of China – a soft thing; how this one had an easy billet in Japan somewhere, and that one was doing well in the Siamese navy; and in all they said – in their actions, in their looks, in their persons could be detected the soft spot, the place of decay, the determination to lounge safely through existence.

The other men that he would occasionally meet in Singapore were the wild-eyed adventurers who were looking for their main chance in the jungles, rivers and remote trading ports of the Eastern Seas. Men who would speak of the vast fortunes they would make in gold mines, diamond mines, coal mines and other ventures in the most remote of locations, and of their alliances with untrustworthy local rulers and vagabonds who were necessary to assist their wild schemes:

> Some, very few and seen there but seldom, led mysterious lives, had preserved an undefaced energy with the temper of buccaneers and the eyes of dreamers. They appeared to live in a crazy maze of plans, hopes, dangers, enterprises, ahead of civilisation, in the dark places of the sea; and their death was the only event of their fantastic existence that seemed to have a reasonable certitude of achievement.

Konrad Korzeniowski had been discharged from the *Highland Forest* in July of 1887 and was recuperating in Singapore. He was a proud sailor, a sailor of sailing ships, a sailor who through hard work had learned the skills of sailing magnificent three-masted barques across the world's oceans to foreign ports and return. For him to look for the easy life and to hire on to a small steam ship and its short passages around the Malay Archipelago was unthinkable. Perhaps because of his injury on *The Highland Forest* he now sought relief from the rigours of sail and took what was for him an easy berth.

The *Vidar* was a coasting steamer of some 400 tons, commanded by a competent, interesting and friendly Scot named David Craig. Konrad was rather lucky to get such a berth. He was in his late twenties, a qualified first mate, but in fact compared to most of his contemporaries he had not been at sea for very long. However, Konrad got along rather well with Captain Craig, who described his first meeting with Konrad in the Shipping Office in

Singapore in August 1887:

> He pleased me at once by his manners, which were
> distinguished and reserved. One of the first things he told
> me was that he was a foreigner by birth, which I had
> already guessed from his accent. I replied that it did not
> matter in the least ... (as it was quite difficult at that time
> to find officers in the East who were not over-fond of the
> bottle).

Konrad found the *Vidar* berthed at the Tanjong Pagar docks, a
squared-off compound of warehouses, coal sheds and workshops.
Coolies streamed in and out of its hold as they loaded goods for
various ports in the Malay Archipelago. Her voyages were short
and confined to local seas and the work proved as light as he
had expected. Through her Konrad came to know the coasts and
people around Borneo as few knew them and to soak them into
his very being.

According to the Singapore and Straits Directory, Syed Mohsin
Bin Salleh Al Joffree was already owner of several steamers in
1883 and had branch houses at Berau and Bulungan. He had four
sons and it was the eldest, Syed Abdulla, who traded on the Berau
River. Also trading there at different times were William Lingard's
agents Charles Olmeijer and Lingard's nephew Jim who became
known as Tuan Jim (Lord Jim):

> It was all one to us who owned the ship. He had to employ
> white men in the shipping part of his business, and many

of those he so employed had never set eyes on him from the first to the last day. I myself saw him but once, quite accidentally on a wharf – an old, dark little man blind in one eye, in a snowy robe and yellow slippers. He was having his hand severely kissed by a crowd of Malay pilgrims to whom he had done some favour in the way of food and money. His alms-giving, I have heard, was most extensive, covering almost the whole Archipelago. For isn't it said that 'The charitable man is the friend of Allah'?

The *Vidar* was a picturesque old steamship with a colourful crew, and its captain, David Craig, was also believed to have a financial interest in the vessel. He had sailed these waters for the last ten or twelve years and knew them like the back of his hand. He not only had to navigate a dangerous archipelago with marauding pirates and treacherous rivers, he also had to deal with the local traders – Dutch, English, Chinese, Arab, Malay and Bugis – in each of these unusual ports. Besides the captain and the first mate, there were two European engineers, a Chinese third engineer, a Malay mate, a ship's crew of eleven Malays, as well as a group of Chinese coolies who worked as deck hands for the loading and unloading of cargo. This was a microcosm of the people of the archipelago and they would all have communicated in Bazaar Malay which was the most commonly used trading language of the region. Already an accomplished linguist, Konrad would have quickly picked up a knowledge of Malay and this would have brought him into direct contact with the people he later describes in his books.

The *Vidar* carried its cargo of commercial goods from Singapore down past the Riau Islands and then through the Carimata Strait into the Java Sea; these were the calm seas that Konrad was seeking. Their first port of call was the river port of Banjarmasin near the entrance to the Barito River in southern Borneo. It teemed with small prows carrying all kinds of goods up and down the river and which also formed a floating market. From there they sailed to the island of Pulau Laut, which was a coaling station lying southeast of the main island of Borneo. Then to the main regional port of Macassar on the south coast of the island of Sulawesi. From there she ran north up the Macassar Strait between Borneo and Sulawesi, stopping at the port of Donggala in Sulawesi before crossing west across the strait to reach the entrance to the Berau River and the trading post at Tanjung Redab established by William Lingard. The *Vidar* would then unload its remaining cargo of commercial goods and was ready to load archipelago goods – such as gutta-percha, rattan, pearl shells, birds' nests, wax and gum-dammar – here and at all the ports on its return voyage to Singapore. Konrad made four voyages to the Berau River in eastern Borneo between August 1887 and January 1888, an experience which he put to lasting use in his novels and short stories. He described the *Vidar* as 'An excellent sea boat, easy internal propulsion, worthy of any man's love. I cherish to this day a profound respect for her memory.'

Konrad's immediate impression was one of contrast. For years he had known the turbulence of the great oceans. Now his voyages were in sunlit seas and among races which, like his own, had retained their pride even though they had been defeated by a colonising power. The Dutch, the English and the Arabs had spread throughout the archipelago and exploited the local Malays, but to Konrad it was the vanquished rather than the newcomers who were exciting, sympathetic and always fascinating. The wheelhouse of the *Vidar* was a great place for conversation to fill in hours of shipboard monotony and Captain Craig would have had many tales from his years in these waters to tell his first officer. Tales of tropical storms at sea, of treacherous rivers and of attacks by pirates. Konrad would also listen to the Malay and Chinese members of the crew and he unconsciously absorbed all the information he could about these various people and the half-concealed enmities which produced clashes between races and religions. Besides this, a varied cast of local traders crowded aboard the *Vidar* at every landing stage of her voyage and provided Conrad with a fascinating cast of characters for his later books. These voyages with their recurring mix of exotic scenery, local traders, local tribesmen and island ports stuck in Konrad's memory and imagination as it seemed that here in Borneo he was on the edge of civilisation.

The Berau River is one of five large rivers on the east coast of Borneo that drain into the Sulawesi Sea. A tidal river with numerous outlets to the sea, the Berau estuary is a maze of channels, sand bars and mudflats matted with mangroves. Its channels are constantly changing and the problem is not to find the entrance to the river but to find which of the many channels is navigable and would join with the main river in the interior. The *Vidar* entered the Berau estuary, found Lingard's Crossing, and as they made their way upstream the mud thickened, the forest closed in, and they came to a village which lined the river. The houses crowded the bank in a close row of bamboo platforms elevated on high poles and the *Vidar* wheezed to a stop at the rickety jetty of Lingard & Company.

The Berau is the main river up from the coast which Conrad named the 'Pantai' in *Almayer's Folly* and *An Outcast of the Islands*, and the 'Patusan' in *Lord Jim*. The settlement of Tanjung Redeb, forty miles up the river, lies on a promontory at the confluence of the Segai River to the north and the Kelai River to the south where they join to form the Berau. William Lingard had set up his office, warehouses and wharf on this promontory. Opposite on the north bank of the Segai is the settlement of Gunung Tabour and the old rajah's palace. Opposite on the east bank of the Kelai is the settlement of Sambaliung, where the Bugis potentate Lakamba had built his stockade and where Syed Abdulla established his wharf and trading post. In *Almayer's Folly,* Conrad provides a description of the settlement:

From the low point of land where Almayer stood he could see both branches of the river. The main stream of the Pantai was lost completely in darkness for the fire at the Rajah's had gone out altogether, but up the Sambir Reach his eye could follow the long line of Malay houses crowding the bank, with here and there a dim light twinkling through bamboo walls, or a smoky torch burning on the platforms built out over the river. Further away, where the island ended in a low cliff, rose a dark mass of buildings towering above the Malay structures. Founded solidly on a firm ground with plenty of space, starred by many lights burning strong and white, with a suggestion of paraffin and lamp-glasses, stood the house and the godowns of Abdulla bin Selim.

Konrad's spell on the *Vidar* served a dual purpose. It restored his health and set his imagination working. In fact, these months would prove crucial in shaping his future, for the places and the people he met became the characters he used in his first books. If they did not actually incline him to write, they at least determined what he would write about and years later he described his life on the *Vidar*:

> It is part of my sea life to which my memory returns most often, since there is nothing to remember but what is good and pleasant. As to the kind of trade she was engaged in and the character of my shipmates, I could not have been happier if I had the life and the men made to my order by a benevolent Enchanter.

Forty miles up the Berau River, the village of Tanjung Redeb is the setting of Conrad's first novels – *Almayer's Folly*, *An Outcast of the Islands* and the second part of *Lord Jim*. In all, he made four voyages to this settlement but managed to have absorbed so much of its setting, and to have met the original characters of his novels, Charles Olmeijer, Carel de Veere and Jim Lingard, as well as the many Arab and Malay characters who people his works.

During his time on the *Vidar*, Konrad Korzeniowski stowed away landscapes, characters and plots that Joseph Conrad unpacked decades later. Altogether, the four and a half months on the *Vidar* inspired more of Conrad's fiction than any other period in his life. He was able to recall not only the different channels in the river and the lushness of the surrounding forest but also the various people of different races and religions, their antecedents, morals, character, intrigues and personal ambitions. And it was this scenery and people that filled the first books of his long literary career.

Charles Olmeijer, a Dutchman born in Java became the principal character of Conrad's first two books - *Almayer's Folly* and *An Outcast of the Islands*. He lived there, much as he is described in the books, as a man whose actual circumstances contrasted with the vastness of his ambition. He made a deep impression on Conrad, who said later: 'If I had not got to know Almayer pretty well, it is almost certain there would never have been a line of mine in print.' For a time, Charles Olmeijer flourished as a local trader but by 1887 the firm's commercial trade had diminished substantially. Conrad describes his first view of Olmeijer in *A Personal Record*:

I had seen him for the first time, some four years before, from the bridge of a steamer moored to a rickety little wharf forty miles up, more or less, a Bornean river. It was very early morning, and barring a small dug-out canoe on the river there was nothing moving within sight. I had just come up yawning from my cabin. The Serang and the

Malay crew were overhauling the cargo chains and trying the winches; their voices sounded subdued on the deck below, and their movements were languid. That tropical daybreak was chilly. The Malay quartermaster, coming up to get something from the lockers on the bridge, shivered visibly. The forests above and below and on the opposite bank looked black and dank; wet dripped from the rigging upon the tightly stretched deck awnings, and it was in the middle of a shuddering yawn that I caught sight of Almayer. He was moving across a patch of burned grass, a blurred shadowy shape with the blurred bulk of a house behind him, a low house of mats, bamboos, and palm leaves, with a high-pitched roof of grass.

He stepped upon the jetty. He was clad simply in flapping pyjamas of crettone pattern (enormous flowers with yellow petals on a disagreeable blue background) and a thin cotton singlet with short sleeves. His arms, bare to the elbow, were crossed on his chest. His black hair looked as if it had not been cut for a very long time, and a curly wisp of it strayed across his forehead.

9

Macassar

Fourscore years ago it was an inconsiderable country but since then has throve mightily by reason of the fairs kept there, for ships met there from Manila, Goa, Macau, both English and Dutch. So that the abundance of rich commodities were brought thither from all parts of the archipelago, and trade enriched the country, making its Sovereign powerful ... No man paid anchorage or any other duty there and saving the presents that captains of ships and merchants of note made to the Sumbane, all the trade was free. This made it the universal mart of these parts of the world.

Friar Domingo Navarette, 1657

From time immemorial, Macassarese traders made annual voyages to the eastern most part of the archipelago, travelling as far as the Aru Islands in the Moluccas and south to Arnhem Land just north of Australia. They followed the monsoonal winds, leaving in December or January at the beginning of the western monsoon and returning in July or August at the onset of the eastern monsoon, in a voyage that took them away from home for nine months. Their aim was to collect pearl shell, turtle shell, trepang or sea cucumber and, most importantly, bird of paradise skins. For collectors, a bird of paradise specimen was worth more than any other bird on the planet and their skins were traded across the world from Macassar. The trepang of Arnhem Land were also highly prized and fetched high prices in Chinese markets. These epic thousand-mile voyages were undertaken in Bugis prahus.

The Bugis prahu was in part a copy of a western schooner of the mid-nineteenth century which traded around the archipelago during that period. It was built without nails or any iron being used. In a time-honoured tradition its shipwrights used only an axe, handsaw, adze and auger to shape and fit the planks of its hull, before the ribs were then added. The boats were built organically, according to the nature of the timber and to a plan that was only in the mind of its master builder.

Malacca, the Portuguese-controlled regional trading centre on the Malay Peninsula was captured by the Dutch East India Company in 1641, and many of the Portuguese and Portuguese Eurasians who lived there then moved to Macassar to continue their pivotal role in Asian trade. Holy relics from the Church of San Domingu de Surian in Malacca were brought to Macassar. At the same time the Malaccan Diocese transferred to Macassar and the Franciscans, the Dominicans and the Jesuits all established houses there, although they were confined to ministering to the Portuguese settlers. The Portuguese were assigned a quarter in the city known as Borrobos, where they were free to settle and practise their religion. In ten years, the Portuguese population in Macassar grew to as many as three thousand out of a total population of fifty thousand.

Macassar was always a thriving regional trading port whose commodities included sandalwood from Timor, sappan dyewood from Sumbawa, pepper, gold and diamonds from Borneo, cloves and nutmeg from the Moluccas, as well as pearls, mother of pearl, tortoise shell, shark fin, and trepang from the eastern islands. Chinese, Arab, Portuguese, Spanish and English merchants frequented the port because the Sultan of Macassar allowed them to trade freely and outside of Dutch control. Up to twenty Portuguese frigates and junks would come to Macassar each year from Goa, Macau and the ports on the Coromandel Coast of India. The Spanish sailed from Manila to Macassar to purchase textiles, gunpowder and saltpetre from India in exchange for silver dollars from Peru. The English East India Company established a warehouse there and reported they could make forty to fifty per cent profit by selling Coromandel textiles in Macassar and investing the proceeds in cloves, tortoise shell, trepang and sandalwood for export to China.

After 1650, when the Dutch East India Company attempted to impose a complete monopoly on the clove and nutmeg trade from the Moluccan islands in easternmost Indonesia, Macassar became a centre for what the Dutch East India Company considered an 'illegal' trade in spices. Macassarese and Bugis traders took rice and foreign goods to the Moluccas to trade for the spices the Dutch were attempting to monopolise. These traders were happy to smuggle the spices from the Moluccas to Macassar where the sultan permitted Portuguese, Spanish, English and Chinese traders to trade freely in his port and where they were beyond

Dutch control.

Of course, the Dutch East India Company was not impressed at having a rival to the trade they controlled from Batavia and Ambon, and at first they sought to influence the sultan by diplomacy and generous gifts. Sultan Hasanuddin had an interest in the sciences and the Dutch East India Company presented him with the latest in scientific knowledge: a set of terrestrial and celestial globes made by Joan Blaeu, as well as a world atlas and a telescope. However, this strategy of diplomacy did not convince the sultan to ban the traders from his port and war appeared to be inevitable.

In 1655, the Dutch demanded that Sultan Hasanuddin expel all foreign traders from his port and that his own merchants should cease trading with those in the Moluccas who were selling cloves and nutmeg in defiance of their self-imposed monopoly. In 1659 the Dutch renewed their demands for the sultan to cease trading with the Moluccas and expel foreign traders. The sultan shrewdly responded that:

> Such prohibition runs counter to the commandment of God, who created the world in order that all mankind should have the enjoyment thereof. Or do you believe that God has reserved these islands, so far away from the place of your nation, for your trade alone?

War appeared inevitable and for good reasons the sultan developed an interest in the techniques of modern warfare and with the help of foreign advisers he set about fortifying his city against attack. The English East India Company factor in Macassar, George Cockayne, wrote in a letter that he was:

> Called every day to the Sultan or else he comes to our house to have me resolve him as well as I can of such questions as he doth propound unto me. The Sultan is much grieved in mind and maketh much preparation for war: all the whole land is making of bricks for two castles this summer to be finished; in the armoury is laid 10,000 lances, 10,000 kris with bucklers (sheaths) for them, spaces (lances) as many, and 2422 pieces (guns) ... Yesterday in my sight the Sultan, to see his force and how many men he could make, at an instant mustered 36,000 able men.

In 1660, two Dutch East India Company ships entered Macassar harbour and proceeded to evacuate their countrymen from the city. It was a signal of what was to come and four days later the main Dutch fleet arrived with thirty-three ships manned by two thousand six hundred soldiers and started their bombardment of the city. Dutch soldiers landed in the southern outskirts of Macassar and successfully seized Fort Panakkukang but were unable to capture the rest of the city. Sultan Hasanuddin pulled down all the houses in front of the Dutch stronghold and erected a battery with fifteen cannons directly opposite the Dutch-occupied fort.

In 1666, the Dutch East India Company formed an informal alliance with Arung Palakka, the former ruler of Bone in South

Sulawesi and his Bugis warriors who were now living in exile on the outskirts of Batavia. Arung Palakka had a mission to redeem his sense of pride and honour after being defeated by his Macassarese overlords and forced into exile. However, it was not until 1669, and after three years of fierce fighting, that Dutch soldiers allied with the Buginese forces finally breached the walls of the sultan's royal citadel in what was described as some of the fiercest fighting experienced by the Dutch East India Company. After the capture, the Dutch built Fort Rotterdam in the standard pentagon style with bastions at each corner and the port was put under direct Dutch rule. It was after the Dutch capture of Macassar and then the adjacent region of Wajo that many of the Bugis traders from Wajo left the island, to seek their fortune in eastern Borneo, in Malaya, in Sumatra and in the Riau Archipelago.

After the collapse into bankruptcy of the Dutch East India Company in 1795 and Singapore's rise in importance as the halfway trading port between West and East in the mid-1800s, Macassar profited from a boom in archipelago commodities. These included pearls, trepang, copra, sandalwood and the famous Macassar Oil which Victorian gentlemen plastered on their hair, obliging their wives to protect the backs of their armchairs with white cloths called anti-macassars. Being far from Dutch rule in Batavia, Macassar was teeming with commerce and it also became a centre for smuggled goods coming into the archipelago including guns, gunpowder and opium. It was the point in the islands where all those non-Dutch foreigners who invaded the Malay Archipelago in search of money and adventure tended to congregate. Bold, reckless, keen in business, making money fast, they used to have a general rendezvous in Macassar for purposes of trade and dissipation. The Dutch merchants called those men English 'pedlars'. Some of them were undoubtedly men for whom that kind of life had a charm, most were seamen and the acknowledged king of them all was William Lingard, whom the Malays, honest or dishonest, quiet fishermen or desperate cut-throats, recognised as 'Rajah Laut' – King of the Sea.

Alfred Russel Wallace arrived in Macassar in 1856 and described the presence of a fine 42-gun Dutch frigate as the guard ship of the place, as well as a small war-steamer and three or four little cutters used for cruising after the pirates which infested these seas and especially on the Borneo coast. There were also a few square-rigged trading vessels in the port and twenty or thirty native prows of various sizes. The town was roughly divided along cultural lines into the European quarter, the Malay quarter and the Bugis quarter, and he described Macassar as:

> Prettier and cleaner than any town I had yet seen in the East. The Dutch have some admirable local regulations. All European houses must be kept well whitewashed, and every person, at four in the afternoon, water the road in front of their house. The streets are kept clear of refuse, and covered drains carry away all the impurities into large open sewers, into which the tide is admitted at high-water and allowed to flow out when it has ebbed.

As witnessed by Wallace, the commercial part of the town consisted of one long narrow street, along the quayside, devoted to businesses and principally occupied by the Dutch and Chinese merchants' offices and warehouses, as well as native shops and an open market. By degrees the brick buildings gave way to bamboo sheds or huts occupied by the Bugis, most of whom were traders dealing in daily necessities such as rice, fish, fruit and fowls. At short distances apart were open shops or workrooms, in which women may be seen weaving the well-known Macassar cloths. Parallel to this street ran two short ones which formed the old Dutch town and were enclosed by gates. These consisted of private houses, and at their southern end was the fort, the church, and a road at right angles to the beach, containing the houses of the governor and of the principle officials. Beyond the fort was a long street of native houses, usually thronged with a native population of Bugis and Macassar men, wearing cotton trousers and the universal Malay sarong of gay checked colours, worn around the waist or across the shoulders.

Konrad Korzeniowski knew Macassar well because it was here that the *Vidar* would unload most of its Singapore merchandise before sailing on to the Berau River to collect archipelago goods from East Borneo. According to Joseph Conrad, a young and slim Charles Almayer, clad all in Dutch colonial white, arrived from Batavia with the Dutch mail-boat to seek his fortune in the port town of Macassar and he soon found a job with Hudig & Company, one of the Dutch trading houses that lined the quay. According to Joseph Conrad it was Tom Lingard who brought the young Peter Willems from Semarang to Macassar where he was able to obtain employment for him with Hudig & Company.

After four voyages from Singapore to the Berau River, Konrad

Korzeniowski decided to sign off from the *Vidar* in January 1888. He probably announced his decision to Captain Craig after they left Macassar and just before they arrived in Singapore. It was time to move on, to move back into sail and in his book *The Shadow-Line* Joseph Conrad describes his conversation with Captain Craig, when he informed him of his decision:

> The Captain stared hard as if wondering what ailed me. But he was a sailor, and he, too, had been young at one time. Presently a smile came to lurk under his thick iron-gray moustache, and he observed that, of course, if I felt I must go he couldn't keep me by main force. And it was arranged that I should be paid off the next morning. As I was going out of his cabin he added suddenly, in a peculiar wistful tone, that he hoped I would find what I was so anxious to go and look for. A soft, cryptic utterance which seemed to reach deeper than any diamond-hard tool could have done. I do believe he understood my case.

The ship's second engineer, a sturdy young Scot with a smooth face and light eyes was a good friend to Konrad. A confirmed bachelor and understood to be a fierce misogynist he had his own explanation as to why his friend was leaving the ship and as described by Conrad:

> His honest red countenance emerged out of the engine-room companion way and then the whole robust man, with shirt sleeves turned up, wiping slowly the massive

fore-arms with a lump of cotton-waste. And his light eyes expressed bitter distaste, as though our friendship had turned to ashes. He said weightily: 'Oh! Aye! I've been thinking it was about time for you to run away home and get married to some silly girl.'

The chief engineer also had a characteristic view of Konrad's action, but in a kindlier spirit. For he was a confirmed dyspeptic and said his case was caused by a deranged liver. He suggested Konrad should stay for another trip and meantime dose himself with a certain patent medicine in which his own belief was absolute:

'I'll tell you what I'll do. I'll buy you two bottles, out of my own pocket. There. I can't say fairer than that, can I?'

10

Voyages of the *Otago*, 1888 - 1889

At first glance I saw that she was a high-class vessel, a
harmonious creature in the lines of her fine body and the
proportioned tallness of her spars. Whatever her age and
history, she had preserved the stamp of her heritage ...
she looked like a creature of high breed – an Arab steed
in a string of cart-horses.

Joseph Conrad, *The Shadow-Line*

Early in 1888 Konrad Korzeniowski lowered himself and his
seabag into a sampan in Singapore Harbour, and was rowed
ashore to Johnstone Pier, from where he took a horse-drawn
cab to Sailors' Home. He had just given up a good berth and a
comfortable life in a fine little steamship with an excellent master.
However, she was not a sailing ship and his ambition was to
command a sailing ship, a square rigger, not in the comfortable
waters of the East Indies, but on the great oceans of the world.
In his introduction to *The Shadow-Line* Conrad describes his

departure from the SS *Vidar*:

Next) day the Captain and I transacted our business in the Harbour Office. It was a lofty, big, cool, white room, where the screened light of day glowed serenely. Everybody in it – the officials, the public – were in white. Only the heavy polished desks gleamed darkly in a central avenue, and some papers lying on them were blue … The official behind the desk we approached grinned amiably and kept it up till, in answer to his perfunctory question, 'Sign off and on again?' my Captain answered, 'No! Signing off for good.' And then his grin vanished in sudden solemnity. He did not look at me again till he handed me my papers with a sorrowful expression, as if they had been my passports for Hades.

While I was putting them away he murmured some question to the Captain, and I heard the latter answer good-humouredly, 'No. He leaves us to go home.'

'Oh!' the other exclaimed, nodding mournfully over my sad condition.

No mail-boat bound for England was due for three or four days and Konrad walked leisurely along the Esplanade towards Sailors' Home. It had the character of a residential club, but with a slightly governmental flavour about it, because it was administered by the Harbour Office. He was ashore for a few days when a message reached him that the harbour master would like to see him urgently. Konrad knew the message must relate to a ship and as he made his way along the waterfront he scanned the Singapore Roads looking for which ship it might be. The harbour master explained that the master of a British ship had died in Bangkok and the consul-general there had cabled to him a request for a competent man to be sent to take command. He gave Konrad an agreement which read:

> This is to inform you that you are required to proceed in the SS *Melita* to Bangkok and you will report your arrival to the British Consul and produce this memorandum which will show that I have engaged you to be the Master of the *Otago*.

After reading its terms, Konrad handed it back to him with the remark that he accepted its conditions. The harbour master signed it, stamped it, folded it in four and presented it to him. Conrad wrote that it seemed as if a pair of wings had suddenly grown on his shoulders:

> And now here I had my command, absolutely in my pocket, in a way undeniable indeed, but most unexpected; beyond my imaginings, outside all reasonable expectations, and even notwithstanding the existence of some sort of obscure intrigue to keep it away from me. It is true that the intrigue was feeble, but it helped the feeling of wonder – as if I had been specially destined for that ship I did not know, by some power higher than the prosaic agencies of the commercial world.

The SS *Melita* was leaving for Bangkok that evening and Konrad would be on it. He arrived in Bangkok on 24 January and as his coastal steamer came up the river its captain was able to point out his new ship. The lines of her fine body and well-proportioned spars pleased Konrad immensely as this was a high-class vessel, a vessel he would be proud to command.

The *Otago* was an iron-hulled barque of about 400 tons which had sailed from Newcastle in New South Wales with a cargo of coal bound for Haiphong in Vietnam. After unloading her coal she sailed for Hong Kong and after leaving there her captain died at sea under unusual circumstances. According to the first mate he had spent the last few weeks of his life in his cabin, not paying the least attention to his ship, playing his violin day and night. One evening, feeling very ill, he had thrown his violin overboard, died, and the following day was buried at sea. The mate then sailed the *Otago* for Bangkok to report the events. It was unlikely that there would be a new master sitting in Bangkok and no doubt the mate had hoped that the owners would simply confirm his acting command for the voyage back to Australia. It seems the mate was recommended only by himself and lacked the necessary master's certificate, whereas Konrad Korzeniowski, sitting in Singapore and waiting for a ship home, happened to have a master's certificate for a square-rigged deepwater sailing ship of the required tonnage. To be offered the command of his first ship was a source of intense excitement and is lyrically evoked in Conrad's writing:

A ship! My ship! She was mine, more absolutely mine for

possession and care than anything in the world; an object of responsibility and devotion. She was there waiting for me, spell-bound, unable to move, to live, to get out into the world (till I came), like an enchanted princess. Her call had come to me as if from the clouds. I had never suspected her existence. I didn't know how she looked, I had barely heard her name, and yet we were indissolubly united for a certain portion of our future, to sink or swim together!

A sudden passion of anxious impatience rushed through my veins, gave me such a sense of the intensity of existence as I have never felt before or since. I discovered how much of a seaman I was, in heart, in mind, and, as it were, physically – a man exclusively of sea and ships; the sea the only world that counted, and the ships, the test of manliness, of temperament, of courage and fidelity – and of love.

In his novel *The Shadow-Line*, Conrad tells the story of a young man who after taking on the responsibility of a ship's captain crosses what he calls 'The Shadow Line' and leaving his youth behind assumes the maturity required for such a position. After putting his feet on deck for the first time Konrad introduces himself to the mate:

In the face of that man, several years, I judged, older than myself, I became aware of what I had left already behind me – my youth. And that was indeed poor comfort. Youth is a fine thing, a mighty power – as long as one does not think of it. I felt I was becoming self-conscious. Almost against my will I assumed a moody gravity. I said: 'I see you have kept her in very good order, Mr. Burns.' The Mate responded by saying 'If I hadn't a wife and a child at home you may be sure, sir, I would have asked you to let me go the very minute you came on board.' I answered him with a matter-of-course calmness as though some remote third person were in question. 'And I, Mr. Burns, would not have let you go. You have signed the ship's articles as chief officer, and till they are terminated at the final port of discharge I shall expect you to attend to your duty and give me the benefit of your experience to the best of your ability.'

All that Konrad could find in the captain's cabin were some unpaid bills and three years of receipts, all in the greatest disorder and thrown into a dusty violin case. It was impossible to find out where the money for the last two cargoes had gone and no trace of it could be found on board the ship. He also learnt from the owners that for more than ten months his predecessor had not even bothered to keep them informed of the ship's movements.

As master of the *Otago*, Konrad was responsible for handling the ship in its more complicated manoeuvres. To control a square-rigged ship, making best use of the available winds, was skilled work, a complex and delicate art. The captain was also responsible for the ship's accounts, disciplined the crew, acted as ship's doctor, supervised rations, kept the ship's official records, often acted as the ship's agent and broker while in port and navigated his vessel through straits, around islands, reefs and all number of marine hazards. The master stood no watch, came and went when he pleased, and was accountable to no one except his owners. He had to be informed of everything of importance that took place on board. He had entire control of the discipline of the ship, so much so that none of the officers under him had any authority to punish a seaman or use any force without the master's order, except only in the cases of urgent necessity.

Konrad immediately encountered problems with sickness amongst the crew, including fever and dysentery. There was consequently some delay in complying with health procedures before the vessel was able to load its cargo and leave port. In 'The Secret Sharer' he describes his first period on the vessel *Otago*:

It must be said, too, that I knew very little of my officers. In consequence of certain events of no particular significance, except to myself, I had been appointed to the command only a fortnight before. Neither did I know much of the hands forward. All these people had been together for eighteen months or so, and my position was that of the only stranger on board. I mention this because it has some bearing on what is to follow. But what I felt most was my being a stranger to the ship; and if all the truth must be told, I was somewhat of a stranger to myself. The youngest man on board (barring the second mate), and untried as yet by a position of the fullest responsibility, I was willing to take the adequacy of the others for granted. They had simply to be equal to their tasks; but I wondered how far I should turn out faithful to that ideal conception of one's own personality every man sets up for himself secretly.

The *Otago* was chartered to load a full cargo of teak logs in Bangkok and sail the thousands of miles to Sydney. Konrad's first role as master was to get the logs aboard. The loading entailed using the ship's heavier tackle and they were probably aided by a few elephants on the wharf to manoeuvre the heavy logs into position. When they got away from the port, down the river and finally out into the open sea, he chose to take the first night watch in order to better understand the ship which was his new command:

I had expected in those solitary hours of the night to get on terms with the ship of which I knew nothing, manned by men of whom I knew very little more. Fast alongside a wharf, littered like any ship in port with a tangle of unrelated things, invaded by unrelated shore people, I had hardly seen her yet properly. Now, as she lay cleared for sea, the stretch of her main-deck seemed to me very fine under the stars. Very fine, very roomy for her size, and very inviting. I descended the poop and paced the waist, my mind picturing to myself the coming passage through the Malay Archipelago and down the Indian Ocean. All its phases were familiar enough to me, every characteristic, all the alternatives which were likely to face me on the high seas – everything! ... except the novel responsibility of command. But I took heart from the reasonable thought that the ship was like other ships, the men like other men, and that the sea was not likely to keep any special surprises expressly for my discomfiture.

Sailing from Bangkok the *Otago* entered the doldrums. For many days there was no proper sailing breeze, Konrad's fine Arabian steed was hobbled by light winds and only able to limp her way southwards. However, the main problem was the persistent sickness among her crew. There had been malaria about in Bangkok and now three members of his small crew needed urgent medical attention. At this point Konrad discovered that the ship's regulation store of quinine, his only weapon against the fever, had been wasted and adulterated by his predecessor. Konrad made the decision to stop in Singapore, where they entered the harbour flying the flag for medical assistance from the mizzen. The *Singapore Free Press* reported on 2 March 1888: 'The British bark *Otago*, bound from Bangkok to Sydney put into port here last evening for medical advice as several of the crew are suffering from fever and the Captain wished to get a further supply of medicine, before he proceeded on his journey. Dr. Mugliston went on board and ordered three of the crew to be sent to hospital. The vessel is outside the Harbour limits.'

After taking on medicine and new crew members, the *Otago* sailed through the Riau Islands to the Java Sea, the Sunda Straits and south through the Indian Ocean to Cape Leeuwin in Western

Australia. To sail the Roaring Forties was challenging, and in a well-run ship an invigorating experience. In *The Mirror of the Sea* Conrad describes crossing the Great Australian Bight with the wind roaring, and the spume and spray flying:

> It was a hard, long gale, grey clouds and green sea, heavy weather undoubtedly, but still what a sailor would call manageable. Under two lower topsails and a reefed foresail the barque seemed to race with a long steady sea that did not becalm her in the troughs. The solemn thundering combers caught up with her from astern, passed with a fierce boiling up of foam level with the bulwarks, swept on ahead with a swish and a roar; and the little vessel, dipping her jib-boom into the tumbling froth, would go running in a smooth glassy hollow, a deep valley between two ridges of sea, hiding the horizon ahead and astern.

The arrival of the *Otago* was reported in *The Sydney Morning Herald* as being under the command of 'Captain Conrad Konkorzentowski' as newspapers invariably misspelled his name. Konrad stayed with the *Otago* and sailed from Sydney to Melbourne to load wheat and then return. The *Otago* was then chartered to sail to Mauritius for a cargo of sugar. In *The Mirror of the Sea,* Conrad gives an account of meeting on the quay in Sydney a second officer with whom he had served as an ordinary seaman on the *Duke of Sutherland*. A man who whenever he went ashore came back to the ship completely drunk:

He recognized me at once, remembered my name, and in what ship I had served under his orders. He looked me over from head to foot. 'What are you doing here?' he asked.

'I am commanding a little barque,' I said, 'loading here for Mauritius.' Then, thoughtlessly, I added, 'And what are you doing?'

'I,' he said, looking at me unflinchingly, with his old sardonic grin – 'I am looking for something to do.'

I felt I would rather have bitten out my tongue. His jet-black, curly hair had turned iron-grey, he was scrupulously neat as ever, but frightfully threadbare. His shiny boots were worn down at heel. But he forgave me, and we drove off together in a hansom cab to dine on board my ship. He went over her conscientiously, praised her heartily and congratulated me on my command with absolute sincerity. At dinner, as I offered him wine and beer he shook his head, and as I sat looking at him interrogatively, he muttered in an undertone: 'I've given up all that.'

After dinner we came again on deck. It seemed as if he could not tear himself away from the ship. We were fitting some new lower rigging accordingly, and he hung about, approving, suggesting, giving me advice in his old manner. Twice he addressed me as 'My boy' and corrected himself quickly to 'Captain' … He said good-bye at last. As I watched his burly, bull-necked figure walk up the street, I wondered with a sinking heart whether he had much more than the price of a night's lodging in his pocket.

Konrad sought the permission of the owners to take the more difficult but more direct route to Mauritius by sailing north through the Torres Strait, rather than trying to beat west in the southern ocean against the prevailing westerlies. As he later wrote in *Last Essays*:

All of a sudden, all the deep-lying historic sense of the exploring ventures in the Pacific surged to the surface of my being. Almost without reflection I sat down and wrote a letter to my owners suggesting that, instead of the usual southern route, I should take the ship to Mauritius by way of the Torres Strait. I ought to have received a severe rap on the knuckles, if only for wasting their time in submitting such an unheard of proposition.

Konrad never expected the owners to agree to his suggestion, but to his great surprise they raised no objection. An additional insurance premium had to be paid for that route but it would also save time at sea. He left Sydney in a terrible south-easterly gale to the great dismay of the pilot and the tugmaster who guided the *Otago* out of the harbour. By choosing to sail through the Torres Strait, Konrad was choosing to sail in the wake of the historic voyages of exploration made by Luís Vaz de Torres in 1606 and Lieutenant James Cook in 1770, as well as the voyage of desperation made by Captain William Bligh after the mutiny on the *Bounty* in 1789. He recalls the voyage with considerable pride:

It was not without a certain emotion that commanding very likely the first, and certainly the last, merchant ship that carried a cargo that way – from Sydney to Mauritius – I put her head at daybreak for Bligh's Entrance, and packed on her every bit of canvas she could carry. Windswept, sunlit empty waters were all around me, half-veiled by a brilliant haze.

... Approaching the other end of the Strait, I sighted a gaunt, grey wreck of a big American ship lying high and dry on the southernmost of Warrior Reefs. She had been there for years. I had heard of her. She was legendary. She loomed up, a sinister and enormous memento mori raised by the refraction of this serene afternoon above the far-away line of the horizon drawn under the sinking sun.

Konrad carefully navigated the *Otago* through the reefs, tides, currents and shallows of the Torres Strait. Some days later they exited through the Endeavour Strait and into the broad reaches of the Arafura Sea:

And thus I passed out of the Torres Strait before the dusk settled on its waters. Just as a clear sun sank ahead of my ship I took a bearing of a little island for a fresh departure, an insignificant crumb of dark earth, lonely, like an advanced sentinel of that mass of broken land and water, to watch the approaches from the side of the Arafura Sea.

With favourable southeast trade winds they reached Mauritius in fifty-four days where he unloaded his cargo. The island, renowned for the scenery of its central mountains and tropical forests, was known as 'The Pearl of the Ocean'. Port Louis had a lazy, unhurried colonial charm and was known for its beauty and the ethnic diversity of its Indo-Mauritian and French Creole population. The ships charterers were Langlois & Company with whom Konrad had frequent contact during his two months in Mauritius. Paul Langlois as quoted by Gerard Jean-Aubrey in *The Sea Dreamer* has provided us with a description of a thirty-one-year-old Konrad:

Forceful and very mobile features, passing very rapidly from gentleness to an agitation bordering on anger. Big black eyes which were as a rule melancholy and dreamy, and gentle as well, except for fairly frequent moments of annoyance. A decisive chin. A beautifully shaped, graceful mouth surmounted by a thick, well-trimmed dark brown moustache.

Konrad enjoyed his time in Port Louis and especially the opportunity to mix with a French-speaking society. His excellent French and perfect manners opened all the local salons to him and he became a frequent guest of the Renouf family. He joined them for tea parties, dinners and carriage rides down the palm-lined avenues of the Jardin des Pamplemousses. For Konrad, who had lived for years without family ties, the Renouf residence and the Renouf family would have been like the home he never had. He seems to have fallen in love with the charming and beautiful twenty-six-year-old Eugénie Renouf, and in his story 'The Planter of Malata' he writes of a young lady who could possibly be a memory of his lost love, the beautiful Eugénie:

'That young lady came and sat down by me. She said: "Are you French, Mr. Renouard?"' He had breathed a whiff of perfume of which he said nothing either – of some perfume he did not know. Her voice was low and distinct. Her shoulders and her bare arms gleamed with an extraordinary splendour, and when she advanced her head into the light he saw the admirable contour of the face, the straight fine nose with delicate nostrils, the exquisite crimson brushstroke of the lips on this oval without colour. The expression of the eyes was lost in a shadowy mysterious play of jet and silver, stirring under the red coppery gold of the hair as though she had been a being made of ivory and precious metals changed into living tissue.

Clearly, they shared a mutual affection, and before leaving Port Louis a love-struck Konrad Korzeniowski asked one of the Renouf brothers for the hand in marriage of Eugénie. Obviously, the family did not regard a sea captain as a suitable match and he was told she was already engaged to marry her cousin, a fact which had not been mentioned by Eugénie in their private conversations. Hurt and heartbroken by this rebuff, Konrad did not pay a farewell visit to the family but sent a polite letter to Gabriel Renouf, saying he would never return to Mauritius and adding that on the day of her wedding his thoughts would be with the couple.

The *Otago* then sailed for Melbourne and Sydney with her cargo of sugar and a few short trips from Sydney to Adelaide to load wheat followed. When the owners requested that Konrad continue in the sugar trade and make a second voyage to Mauritius, he refused to return and signed off from the *Otago* in March 1889. He departed for England by passenger steamer and before leaving Adelaide he was pleased to receive a letter of recommendation from the owners:

> Referring to your resignation of the command ... of our barque *Otago*, we now have much pleasure in stating that this early severance from our employ is entirely at your own desire, with a view to visiting Europe, and that we entertain a high opinion of your ability in the capacity you now vacate.

After Konrad returned from Australia, he took rooms in a furnished apartment on a Pimlico square and waited for another command. The book *Almayer's Folly* began in the front sitting-room of Joseph Conrad's furnished apartment on an autumn day in September 1889. With no ship and no immediate prospect of another command his days were empty and he began to write. He remembers somewhat lyrically that it was an autumn day with an opaline atmosphere, a veiled, semi-opaque, lustrous day, with fiery points and flashes of red sunlight on the roofs and the windows opposite, while the trees of the square with all their leaves gone were like tracings of Indian ink on a sheet of tissue paper.

11

Voyage into the
Heart of Darkness, 1890

I was fascinated. It was as though a veil had been rent. I saw on
that ivory face the expression of sombre pride, of ruthless power,
of craven terror – of an intense and hopeless despair. Did he live
his life again in every detail of desire, temptation, and surrender
during that supreme moment of complete knowledge? He cried
in a whisper at some image, at some vision – he cried out twice,
a cry that was no more than a breath:

"The horror! The horror!"

Joseph Conrad, *Heart of Darkness*

Knowing Józef Konrad's love of tall ships and the world's oceans,
it seems inconceivable that he would volunteer to take command
of a riverboat in the Upper Congo. To voyage with a paddleboat
up one of the world's major rivers requires its captain to have a
detailed knowledge of its channels, shallows, sand banks, rocky
gorges and its conditions under flood or when dry. For someone

like Konrad, who was a deepwater sailor, skilled in handling three-masted sailing clippers, this was a most unusual choice. However, Africa was fascinating for the young Józef and he explains in his autobiography how he could not resist the opportunity to penetrate its very heart:

It was in 1868, when nine years old or thereabouts, that while looking at a map of Africa of the time and putting my finger on the blank space then representing the unsolved mystery of that continent, I said to myself with absolute assurance and an amazing audacity which are no longer in my character now:

'When I grow up I shall go there.'

And of course I thought no more about it till after a quarter of a century or so an opportunity offered to go there – as if the sin of childish audacity were to be visited on my mature head. Yes. I did go there: *there* being the region of Stanley Falls, which in 1868 was the blankest of blank spaces on the earth's figured surface.

In 1890, at the age of thirty-two, Konrad was appointed by the Belgian Limited Company for Trade on the Upper Congo to serve on one of its riverboats. He left Bordeaux on a French steamship in May 1890 and arrived at Bomo, sixty miles upriver from the mouth of the River Congo, a month later. He then sailed another thirty miles to Matadi which is the highest navigable point of the lower Congo River, because between Kinshasa and Matadi the mighty river narrows and falls through a number of cataracts and deep canyons which make it unnavigable. Konrad spent a fortnight there and saw the company blasting rock and moving dirt for the first stage of the planned Matadi to Kinshasa railway. This railway took eight years to build, cost more than three times as much as the original budget and became the death knell for the one in five workers, who died from sickness and exhaustion. It was here that Konrad first witnessed the company's brutal methods of operation and its use of black slave labour, as described in *Heart of Darkness*:

A slight clinking behind me made me turn my head. Six black men advanced in a file, toiling up the path. They walked erect and slow, balancing small baskets full of earth on their heads, and the clink kept time with their footsteps. Black rags were wound round their loins, and the short ends behind waggled to and fro like tails. I could see every rib, the joints of their limbs were like knots in a rope; each had an iron collar on his neck, and all were connected together with a chain whose bights swung between them, rhythmically clinking ... All their meagre breasts panted together, the violently dilated nostrils quivered, the eyes stared stonily uphill. They passed me within six inches, without a glance, with that complete, deathlike indifference.

Konrad then joined a caravan of sixty porters on an overland trek of about two hundred miles to Kinshasa. These porters, or human beasts of burden, were hauling or carrying, section by section, parts of a small steamer which was to be re-assembled in Kinshasa for further exploration of the mighty river Congo and its tributaries. He saw first-hand the conditions of the natives forced to carry and haul sections of the river steamers and their dead bodies which lay unburied beside the path. When he finally arrived in Kinshasa, Konrad found that the steamer he had been employed to command had been wrecked and he was forced to join the river steamer *Roi des Belges* as an understudy to its captain on the voyage. While travelling upriver the captain became seriously ill. Konrad assumed command and although himself also ill with fever and dysentery he guided the vessel to the company's innermost trading station which was one thousand miles further upstream at Stanley Falls:

> Going up that river was like traveling back to the earliest beginnings of the world, when vegetation rioted on the earth and the big trees were kings. An empty stream, a great silence, an impenetrable forest. The air was warm, thick, heavy, sluggish. There was no joy in the brilliance of sunshine. The long stretches of the waterway ran on, deserted, into the gloom of overshadowed distances. On silvery sand-banks hippos and alligators sunned themselves side by side. The broadening waters flowed through a mob of wooded islands; you lost your way on that river as you would in a desert, and butted all day long against shoals, trying to find the channel, till you thought yourself bewitched and cut off for ever from everything you had known once – somewhere – far away

– in another existence perhaps.

In his journey up the river, he saw the suffering of the black slaves and the cruelty of the white colonialists exploiting Africa. The voyage left him physically ill with malarial fever, dysentery and psychologically disillusioned because of what he had seen and experienced. The Belgian company was in the Congo to make money, the only money to be made was in the ivory trade, Stanley Falls was its epicentre and his protagonist Kurtz was its master:

Ivory? I should think so. Heaps of it, stacks of it. The old mud shanty was bursting with it. You would think there was not a single tusk left either above or below the ground in the whole country. 'Mostly fossil,' the manager had remarked, disparagingly. It was no more fossil than I am; but they call it fossil when it is dug up. It appears the natives do bury the tusks sometimes – but evidently they couldn't bury this parcel deep enough to save the gifted Mr. Kurtz from his fate. We filled the steamboat with it, and had to pile a lot on the deck. Thus he could see and enjoy as long as he could see, because the appreciation of this favour had remained with him to the last. You should have heard him say, 'My ivory.' Oh, yes, I heard him. 'My Intended, my ivory, my station, my river, my –' everything belonged to him.

As witness to the naked greed of the white masters and their ruthless disregard for the native peoples, Konrad gained one of his most famous books which was *Heart of Darkness,* in what he described as the vilest scramble for loot that ever disfigured the history of human conscience and geographical exploration. His protagonist Kurtz represents both good and evil, but according to Konrad it is his remote location and distance from civilisation that releases his primitive evil self.

Due to the illnesses he contracted on the Congo River and his determination to get himself out of there, Konrad Korzeniowski broke his contract after completing only five months of his three-year assignment in the service of the Belgian company. He returned from the Belgian Congo to London in January 1891, physically sick, mentally dispirited and with a profound nervous depression. He spent weeks in an English hospital trying to recover and then a month in a Swiss health clinic. Still unable to go to sea he took a temporary job as a warehouse manager which he considered as penal servitude. He continued to work on the manuscript of *Almayer's Folly* during this period of recovery and added more chapters to his narrative. After eight months of relative inactivity, he was fortunate to find a position as chief officer on the sailing ship *Torrens* in November 1891. Konrad had known its captain, WH Cope, socially, and he wrote:

I had known him some years before, but only slightly, in a social way. I knew that he had been a Conway boy, that he had had much varied service in mail boats, and in the Hooghly pilot steamer before the command of the *Torrens* came his way. But I had no reason to believe that he remembered me particularly. However on hearing from his brother that

I was ashore, he sent me word that the *Torrens* wanted a chief officer, as a matter that might interest me. I was then recovering slowly from a bad break-down, after a most unpleasant and persistent tropical disease which I had caught in Africa while commanding a steamer on the River Congo. Yet the temptation was great. I confessed to him my doubts about my fitness for the post, from the point of view of my health. But he said that moping ashore never did anyone any good and was very encouraging.

The position of chief officer was a step down in rank for a man who had qualified to be a captain, but Konrad accepted the position because of the prestige of the ship and because he was convinced that the only cure for his nervous breakdown and for his general health was to be once more at sea.

12

Voyages of the *Torrens*, 1891-1893

The *Torrens* was a magnificent clipper of about twelve hundred tons, a fully rigged ship with good lines which sailed well. Built in 1875 in Sunderland, she was a 'composite ship' and consisted of stout wooden planks bolted onto an iron frame. Built for the Australian wool trade – London to Adelaide for the February wool sales and return by way of the Cape of Good Hope. She was one of the best and fastest sailing ships ever built and set an unbroken record by sailing from Plymouth to Adelaide in sixty-four days. For Konrad's first voyage she would have sailed from New South Dock in London, and in *The Mirror of the Sea* he describes the dock during the days of the wool clippers:

> To a man who has never seen the extraordinary nobility, strength, and grace that the devoted generations of shipbuilders have evolved from some pure nooks of their simple souls, the sight that could be seen five–and-twenty years ago of a large fleet of clippers moored along the north side of the New South Dock was an inspiring spectacle. Then there was a quarter of a mile of them,

from the iron dockyard gates guarded by policemen, in a long, forest-like perspective of masts, moored to stout wooden jetties. Their spars dwarfed with their loftiness the corrugated iron sheds, their jibbooms extended far over the shore, their white and gold figure-heads, almost dazzling in their purity, overhung the straight, long quay above the mud and dirt of the wharfside, with the busy figures of groups and single men moving to and fro, restless and grimy under their soaring immobility.

To serve in a ship like this, even as chief officer, was a great opportunity. The *Torrens* also carried passengers and was clearly aimed at the upper end of the travel market as she carried only first- and second-class passengers. The voyages served to restore Konrad's health and he served on two round voyages to Australia from 1891 until 1893. He enjoyed the long passages, the sunny trade winds and the rush of the Roaring Forties. After his service in the *Torrens* he paid her this special tribute:

Apart from her more brilliant qualities, such as her speed and her celebrated good looks, she was regarded as a 'comfortable ship' ... which means that she was known to handle easily and to be a good sea boat in heavy weather ... and I can testify that, on every point of sailing, the way that ship had of letting big seas slip under her did one's heart good to watch. It resembled so much an exhibition of intelligent grace and unerring skill that it could fascinate even the least seamanlike of our passengers.

The work of handling the great acreages of sail was very heavy, even for men and boys with a strong constitution. Working aloft was always dangerous as it required balancing on the footlines. When hauling sail up or down while the wind blew, the ship rolled and the masts swung from side to side. It was certainly not a job for the faint-hearted.

While aboard, Konrad continued to work on *Almayer's Folly* and had his first reader on the outward voyage of the *Torrens*. William Jacques, frail, literate and fresh from university became the first ever reader of a Joseph Conrad story when the author asked him if he would read the eight chapters of his manuscript. As described in *A Personal Record*:

'Would it bore you very much reading a manuscript in a handwriting like mine?' I asked him one evening on a sudden impulse at the end of a longish conversation whose subject was Gibbon's History. Jacques was sitting in my cabin one stormy dog-watch below, after bringing me a book to read from his own travelling store.

'What is this?'

'It is a sort of a tale,' I answered with an effort. 'It is not even finished yet. Nevertheless I would like to know what you think of it.'

He put the manuscript, in the breast pocket of his jacket; I remember perfectly his thin brown fingers folding it lengthwise. 'I will read it tomorrow,' he remarked, seizing the door handle, and then, watching the roll of the ship for a propitious moment, he opened the door and was gone.

Next day, but this time in the first dog-watch, Jacques entered my cabin. He had a thick, woollen muffler round his throat and the manuscript was in his hand. He tendered it to me with a steady look but without a word. I took it in silence. He sat down on the couch and still said nothing. I opened and shut a drawer under my desk, on which a filled-up log-slate lay wide open in its wooden frame waiting to be copied neatly into the sort of book I was accustomed to write with care, the ship's log-book. I turned my back squarely on the desk. And even then Jacques never offered a word. 'Well, what do you say?' I asked at last. 'Is it worth finishing?' This question expressed exactly the whole of my thoughts.

'Distinctly,' he answered in his sedate, veiled voice and then coughed a little.

'Were you interested?' I inquired further almost in a whisper.

'Very much!'

'Now let me ask you one more thing: is the story quite clear to you as it stands?'

He raised his dark, gentle eyes to my face and seemed surprised. 'Yes! Perfectly.'

This was all I was to hear from his lips concerning the merits of *Almayer's Folly*. We never spoke together of the book again. A long period of bad weather set in and I had no thoughts left but for my duties, whilst poor Jacques caught a fatal cold and had to keep close in his cabin. The purpose instilled into me by his simple and final 'Distinctly' remained dormant, yet alive to await its opportunity.

Once the ship arrived in Adelaide it was all about wool. Everywhere there were huge bales of wool, brought down from the back blocks and piled in great stacks in the warehouses before they could be transferred to the *Torrens* for the return voyage. One of the passengers on the return leg from Adelaide to London was the young John Galsworthy who was planning to be a lawyer, not a writer, and was returning from a journey attempting to meet Robert Louis Stevenson in the South Seas. Galsworthy grew intrigued by the dark-haired, bearded officer's 'tales of ships and storms, of Polish revolution ... of the Malay seas and the Congo', stories that were so different from his own privileged background. They would become friends for life and this friendship was to be of great help to Conrad in his subsequent writing career. Galsworthy later wrote his impression of the chief officer:

The chief mate bears the main burden of a sailing ship. All of the first night he was fighting a fire in the hold. It was he who had most truck with the tail of a hurricane off Leeuwin and later with another storm. A good seaman, watchful of the weather, quick in handling the ship; considerate with the apprentices – we had a long unhappy Belgian youth among them who dreaded going aloft. Conrad compassionately spared him all he could. With the crew he was popular; they were individuals to him, not a mere gang; and long after he would talk of this or that among them.

... On that ship he told of life not literature. On my last evening he asked me at the Cape to his cabin, and I remember feeling that he outweighed for me all the other experiences of the voyage. Fascination was Conrad's great characteristic – the fascination of vivid expressiveness and zest, of his deep affectionate heart, and his far-ranging, subtle mind. He was extraordinarily perceptive and receptive.

Captain Cope was considering transferring to steam and there seemed a chance that Konrad might succeed him as captain of the *Torrens*. It was a position he would have welcomed, but in the end it did not happen. On the 15th of October 1893 he disembarked at New South Dock in London. While walking down the quay he turned to take a long look at the *Torrens*, unaware that she would be the last of the three-masted barques on which he was to serve. Stepping around the corner of a tall warehouse, he parted from her and his life on sailing ships forever.

The *Torrens* was such a beautiful ship that when she was taken to Genoa to be broken up at the end of her service the Genoese shipwrights were so moved by the beauty of her lines and the perfection of her build that they had no heart to break her up and instead they went to work to preserve her life for a few more years. Conrad was glad that she escaped the ignominious fate of being laid up as a coal hulk and when her sea service finally ended, he wrote his own loving memorial:

But in the end her body of iron and wood, so fair to look upon had to be broken up – I hope with fitting reverence; and as I sit here, thirty years, almost to the day, since I last set eyes upon her, I love to think that her perfect form found a merciful end on the sunlit sea of my boyhood's dreams, and that her fine spirit has returned to dwell in the regions of the great winds, the inspirers and the companions of her swift, renowned, sea-tossed life, which I, too, have been permitted to share for a little while.

13

Voyage of the *Adowa*, 1893

Indubitably it was a Company, it even had a house flag, all white with the letters F. C. T. C. artfully tangled up in a complicated monogram. We flew it at our main-masthead, and now I have come to the conclusion that it was the only flag of its kind in existence.

Joseph Conrad, *A Personal Record*.

Without a posting and in London with time on his hands, Konrad would spend his afternoons walking the streets of the capital and at about five o'clock in the evening find his way to the rooms of the London Shipmasters' Society on Fenchurch Street. The rooms which were full of men, tobacco smoke and sea stories became a sort of haven where his spirit, longing for the sea, could feel itself nearer to the ships and the life of his choice. Conrad writes in his *Personal Record* of a meeting with a Captain Froud at the rooms in November 1893:

Thus, one murky November afternoon he beckoned me in with a crooked finger and that peculiar glance above his spectacles which is perhaps my strongest physical recollection of the man. 'I have had in here a shipmaster, this morning,' he said, getting back to his desk and motioning me to a chair, 'who is in want of an officer. It's for a steamship. You know, nothing pleases me more than to be asked, but, unfortunately, I do not quite see my way ...'

As the outer room was full of men, I cast a wondering glance at the closed door; but he shook his head.

'Oh, yes, I should be only too glad to get that berth for one of them. But the fact of the matter is, the captain of that ship wants an officer who can speak French fluently, and that's not so easy to find. I do not know anybody myself but you. It's a second officer's berth and, of course, you would not care ... would you now? I know that it isn't what you are looking for.'

It was not. But Konrad was without work and Captain Froud explained that the steamship *Adowa* had been chartered by a French company intending to establish a regular monthly line of sailings from Rouen for the transport of French emigrants to Canada. The next day Konrad was interviewed by the captain who explained that his chief mate was an excellent man in every respect and that he could not think of dismissing him so as to give Konrad the higher position, but that if he consented to come as second officer he would be given certain special advantages ...

and so on ... and so on.

Konrad was under the impression the Franco-Canadian Transport Company was the owner of a large fleet with fortnightly departures for Montreal and Quebec as advertised in the pamphlets and prospectuses which came aboard in a large package. Industrious London carpenters had laboured for weeks installing four hundred and sixty bunks for potential emigrants, while the *Adowa* lay at Victoria Docks. She then departed for Rouen to collect her passengers, while proudly flying the house-flag which was all white with the letters FCTC which Conrad describes as artfully tangled up in a complicated monogram. The arrival of the *Adowa* was celebrated in Rouen and all the street corners were plastered with Tricolour posters announcing the birth of the FCTC Company. Soon the Directors of the Company arrived from Paris for a tour of inspection which left Konrad with some feeling of disquiet:

Some gentlemen from Paris – I think there were three of them, and one was said to be the chairman – turned up, indeed, and went from end to end of the ship, knocking their silk hats cruelly against the deck beams. I attended them personally, and I can vouch for it that the interest they took in things was intelligent enough, though, obviously, they had never seen anything of the sort before. Their faces as they went ashore wore a cheerfully inconclusive expression. Notwithstanding that this inspecting ceremony was supposed to be a preliminary to immediate sailing, it was then, as they filed down our gangway, that I received the inward notion that no sailing within the meaning of our charter party would ever take place.

The ship was ready to depart but no passengers arrived. Sometime after the departure of the company directors the ship was moved from its mooring in the neighbourhood of the Opera House to an altogether muddier and shabbier location with a background of grimy houses across from a wide stretch of paved quay, brown with frozen mud. After waiting a few more weeks the emigrants still never came forward and it seems that in the meantime the company had collapsed. According to Conrad:

This was the end of the short-lived, but ephemeral Franco-Canadian Transport Company. A death leaves something behind, but there was never anything tangible left from the F.C.T.C. It flourished no longer than roses live, and unlike the roses it blossomed in the dead of winter, emitted a sort of faint perfume of adventure, and died before spring set in.

Waiting in Rouen, Conrad transported his imagination back to Borneo and the Berau River. In *A Personal Record* he describes working on the tenth chapter of *Almayer's Folly*:

I remember tracing these words of Almayer's romantic daughter on the gray paper of a pad which rested on the blanket of my bed-place. "It has set at last,' said Nina to her mother, pointing to the hills behind which the sun had sunk. "Listen, mother, I am going now to Bulangi's creek, and if I should never return ..." The words referred to a sunset in the Malayan Isles and shaped themselves in my mind, in a hallucinated vision of forests and rivers and seas, far removed from this commercial and yet romantic town of the northern hemisphere.

The *Adowa* returned from Rouen for London and on 17 January 1894, Konrad Korzeniowski disembarked and unknowingly ended his service at sea. Within a few weeks of his return a telegram arrived from Ukraine informing him of 'the sad and painful news of the death of your uncle ... the late Tadeusz Bobrowski.' Uncle Tadeusz, the man who had helped him through his education and early career, his substitute father, had gone. Death had taken from Konrad a being whom he loved deeply, the man who had cared for him in his childhood, watched over his adolescence, contributed to his success and, through the years of his sea life, whether near to him or far, had never ceased to show him constant benevolent affection. Ten years later Conrad wrote:

I cannot speak of Thadeus Bobrowski, my uncle, tutor and benefactor, without emotion. To this very day, after ten years, I still have the feeling of a terrible bereavement. He was a man of great character and remarkable intelligence. He did not understand my desire for the sea, but he did not oppose it on principle. In the course of my twenty years of wandering, I saw him only four times, but I owe the good sides of my character to his affection, protection and influence.

In 1894, aged thirty-six, Konrad Korzeniowski reluctantly gave up the sea, partly because of poor health, partly due to the unavailability of ships, and partly because he had become fascinated with writing. Konrad's lack of a ship meant that he could now devote his full attention to completing the manuscript of *Almayer's Folly* which he had been working on for the last five years.

14

From Konrad Korzeniowski to Joseph Conrad

Until I began to write that novel I had written nothing but letters, and not very many of these. I never made a note of a fact, of an impression, or of an anecdote in my life. The conception of a planned book was entirely outside my mental range.

Joseph Conrad, *A Personal Record*

Konrad had returned to London from Australia in 1889 after an absence of two and a half years while sailing the *Otago* on the eastern seas and took a room at Bessborough Gardens in Pimlico. Idle in London he began to write and the characters he had met on the Berau River began to visit him. As he wrote in *A Personal Record*:

It was in the front sitting-room of furnished apartments in a Pimlico square that they first began to live again with a vividness and poignancy quite foreign to our former real intercourse. I had been treating myself to a long stay on shore, and in the necessity of occupying my mornings, Almayer (that old acquaintance) came nobly to the rescue. Before long, as was only proper, his wife and daughter joined him round my table and then the rest of that Pantai band came full of words and gestures. Unknown to my respectable landlady, it was my practice directly after my breakfast to hold animated receptions of Malays, Arabs and half-castes. They did not clamour aloud for my attention. They came with a silent and irresistible appeal – and the appeal, I affirm here, was not to my self-love or my vanity. It seems now to have had a moral character, for why should the memory of these beings, seen in their obscure sun-bathed existence, demand to express itself in the shape of a novel, except on the ground of that mysterious fellowship which unites in a community of hopes and fears all the dwellers on this earth?

Over the next five years he continued to work on his story and the manuscript travelled with him up the River Congo, to Australia and back on the *Torrens*, to Rouen and back on the *Adowa* and to Poland where it was nearly lost at a railway station in Berlin. He wrote in *A Personal Record*:

When I sat down to write; the ambition of being an author had never turned up among those gracious imaginary existences one creates fondly for oneself at times in the stillness and immobility of a day-dream: yet it stands clear as the sun at noonday that from the moment I had done blackening over the first manuscript page of *Almayer's Folly*, from the moment I had, in the simplicity of my heart and the amazing ignorance of my mind, written that page the die was cast. Never had Rubicon been more blindly forded without invocation to the gods, without fear of men.

Conrad could have written in Polish, French or English but the fact that he wrote in English, which was probably his fourth language since he would have learnt some Russian, caused some surprise and even some criticism early in his writing career. But as explained by Conrad:

The truth of the matter is that my faculty to write in English is as natural as any other aptitude with which I might have been born. I have a strange and overpowering feeling that it had always been an inherent part of myself, English for me was neither a matter of choice nor adoption. The merest idea of a choice had never entered my head. And as to adoption – well yes, there was an adoption; but it was I who was adopted by the genius of the language, which directly I came out of the stammering stage made me its own so completely that its very idioms I truly believe had a direct action on my temperament and fashioned my still plastic character.

In *A Personal Record* he describes writing the tenth chapter of *Almayer's Folly* on board the *Adowa* in Rouen harbour. The remaining two chapters, which brought his novel to its fatal conclusion, were completed in only three months and on 22 May 1894 he sent it off to a publisher. His choice of potential publisher was T. Fisher Unwin, a patron of letters and of considerable reputation. Conrad said that 'Acceptance, came some three months later, in the first typewritten letter I ever received in my life.' He could scarcely have realised his own good fortune, that a first work, even of originality and merit, would be immediately accepted. An extremely unusual event and had he been more familiar with the world of publishing he would have recognised this as a miracle.

Every miracle needs a miracle-worker and this person was Edward Garnett, a man younger than Conrad and a professional reader who was then advising Fisher Unwin. Garnett immediately recognised the rare quality of Conrad's work. It is easy enough to see why now, after his twenty novels, but at that time it was remarkable. A reader is not always interested in the identity of the writer but Edward Garnett was particularly intrigued in the identity of this new voice. The strangeness of the tropical atmosphere, the poetic realism of his romantic story, made him think he must be of eastern origin. No doubt he was quite surprised to meet a thirty-eight-year-old master mariner of Polish birth.

Conrad had spent five years writing *Almayer's Folly* and the book was never dismissed from his mind, even during his voyage up the River Congo or while he was on a visit to his uncle in Poland. His book is about Kaspar Almayer, a man who betrays his own integrity, because he accepts Lingard's promise of his inheritance on the condition that he marries his adopted daughter. It is from this initial mistake that follow all his later woes, culminating in his desertion by his own daughter. All the hallmarks of Conrad's fiction are stamped on the opening pages. The alienation of the individual, the uncaring brutality of the natural world, the serpentine sentences which begin with close observation and finish with a flourish of dark rhetoric. From the opening sentences when Almayer stands on his verandah watching the river swollen with rain, a reader will know they are in the presence of a writer blessed with astonishing ability:

> One of those drifting trees grounded on the shelving shore, just by the house, and Almayer, neglecting his dream, watched it with languid interest. The tree swung slowly round, amid the hiss and foam of the water, and soon getting free of the obstructions began to move downstream again, rolling slowly over, raising upward a long, denuded branch, like a hand lifted in mute appeal to heaven against the river's brutal and unnecessary violence. Almayer's interest in the fate of the tree increased rapidly. He leaned over to see if it cleared the low point below. It did; then he drew back, thinking that now its course was free down to the sea, and he envied the lot of that inanimate thing now growing small and indistinct in the deepening darkness.

Almayer's Folly was published in April 1895 and its appearance marked Konrad's first use of the pen name 'Joseph

Conrad'. It met with extraordinary critical acclaim for a first novel by a wholly unknown author although it had little popular success. At this time Conrad still thought of himself as a seaman who could write, rather than a writer with sailing experience and after the long gestation of *Almayer's Folly* he did not know if he had enough patience to complete another book. However, the rich material of his life at sea meant that seldom would he have to meet a writer's common problem: the lack of a plot. Conrad's mastery of narrative detail depended upon memory and he could, when the need arose, re-create a substantial fragment of autobiography. It was, in fact, a visual memory, to which was added the most important gift for a writer which is perseverance.

What made *Almayer's Folly* different was that it was a story written in English that had for that time a very un-English perspective. There was no romantic hero, there was no love story, it was based outside England but there was no idea of Empire. Its protagonist, Kaspar Almayer, was not an Englishman but a Dutchman. He is introduced as a man who despite his dreams of grandeur is a failure, an anti-hero, and the narrative does not follow what would usually be his restoration to glory but his slow descent into complete failure and finally opium addiction.

At the peak of Empire and of imperial grandeur an Englishman of that era would have no reason to questions his assumption of individual and national self-sufficiency and superiority, he would take it all for granted. Conrad, however, could take very little for granted. Taught by his early acquaintance with deprivation and insecurity he knew how much humans depend on what is external to the self, yet how little we can control it. For this reason his books are more like Shakespearean tragedies than anything else written at that time.

For twenty years he had voyaged across almost every ocean on the globe. He had visited the Caribbean, the northern republics of Latin America, and travelled regularly to India, Singapore, the Dutch East Indies and Australia. Through his life and his travels he had a strong sense of the relativity of identity and cultures, having himself visited the further regions of the world. And he had even penetrated into what were thought of as the darkest places on earth: Borneo and the Congo. Thus, when he wrote his first novel he had no doubt that human beings were born into a condition of insecurity, and as he wrote in the Author's Note to *Almayer's Folly*:

> I am content to sympathise with common mortals, no matter where they live, in houses or in huts, in the streets under a fog, or in the forests behind the dark line of dismal mangroves that fringe the vast solitude of the sea. For, their land – like ours – lies under the inscrutable eyes of the Most High, their hearts like ours – must endure the load of gifts from Heaven, the curse of facts and the blessings of illusions, the bitterness of our wisdom and the deceptive consolation of our folly.

Himself a victim of Russian imperialism, he remained deeply sceptical of any justification for the spread of imperialism, and despite the fact that his contact with foreign people was necessarily superficial he never failed to acknowledge that their lives were just as important as his own. Conrad said that his desire to write 'was a hidden obscure necessity, a completely masked and unaccountable phenomenon' which was to follow those storytellers that as a young boy had captured his imagination, and he writes in *A Personal Record* that:

> Only in men's imagination does every truth find an effective and undeniable existence. Imagination, not invention, is the supreme master of art as of life. An imaginative and exact rendering of authentic memories may serve worthily that spirit of piety towards all things human which sanction the conception of a writer of tales, and the emotions of the man reviewing his own experience.

The fact that his first book almost immediately met with extraordinary critical acclaim, would have certainly started him thinking about another book and Conrad credits Edward Garnett for giving him the permission to continue writing:

> One evening when we had dined together and he had listened to an account of my perplexities he pointed out that there was no need to determine my future absolutely. Then he added "You have the style, you have the temperament; why not write another?" I believe that as far as one man may wish to influence another man's life Edward Garnett had a great desire that I go on writing ... At about eleven o'clock of a nice London night, Edward

and I walked along interminable streets talking of many things, and I remember that on getting home I sat down and wrote about half a page of *An Outcast of the Islands* before I slept.

Joseph Conrad's imagination returned to the Berau River and it was a dinner invitation from Charles Olmeijer that introduced him to another of his flawed anti-heroes, the young Dutchman Carel de Veere. During the dinner, De Vere sat silently at the table and an air of futile mystery hung over him. In his Author's Note to *An Outcaste of the Islands* Conrad wrote that:

The very first time he and Captain Craig dined with Olmeijer there was Carel de Veere sitting at table with us in the manner of the skeleton at the feast, obviously shunned by everybody, never addressed by anyone, and for all recognition of his existence getting now and then from Olmeijer a venomous glance which I observed with great surprise. In the course of the whole evening he ventured one single remark which I didn't catch because his articulation was imperfect, as of a man who had forgotten how to speak. I was the only person who seemed aware of the sound. De Veere subsided. Presently he retired, pointedly unnoticed – into the forest maybe? Its immensity was there, within three hundred yards of the verandah, ready to swallow up anything. Olmeijer conversing with my captain did not stop talking while he glared angrily at the retreating back. Didn't that fellow bring the Arabs into the river!

Nevertheless, De Veere turned up next morning on Olmeijer's verandah. From the bridge of the steamer Conrad could plainly see these two, breakfasting together, one with his air of being no longer interested in the world and the other raising his eyes now and then with intense dislike. Despite their apparent animosity it seems that Charles Olmeijer was happy to talk to someone, anyone, in the Dutch language.

In *An Outcast of the Islands,* Carel de Veere becomes Peter Willems, who as Conrad writes is the victim of his own illusions and his search for material gratification. Finally, it his obsession with the beautiful and exotic Aissa that causes him to allow the Arabs into the river.

The words came easily and only a few months after the publication of *Almayer's Folly* Conrad was able to announce to Garnett in September 1985, the 'death of Mr Peter Willems late of Rotterdam and Macassar murdered on the 16th instant at 4pm.' *An Outcast of the Islands* was published six months later in March 1896 by T. Fisher Unwin. An unsigned review in the *Saturday Review* recognised Conrad as a great novelist, stating that:

> Mr Conrad is wordy; his story is not so much told as seen intermittently through a haze of sentences. His style is like river-mist; for a space things are seen clearly, and then comes a great grey bank of printed matter, page on page, creeping around the reader, swallowing him up …

Then suddenly things loom up again, and in a moment become real, intense, swift.

Joseph Conrad knew this was a serious review that could do him nothing but good, especially with him struggling with his next novel *The Rescue*, which was giving him great difficulty. He was curious as to who the author of the review was and wrote excitedly to Edward Garnett:

I wrote to the reviewer. I did! And he wrote to me. He did! And who do you think it is? – He lives in Woking. Guess. Can't tell – I will tell you. It is H.G. Wells. May I be cremated alive like a miserable moth if I suspected it. Anyway he descended from his 'Time Machine' to be as kind as he knew how.

In 1896 Joseph Conrad married Jessie George and his life changed completely. It was no longer a lonely existence of living on ships or in boarding houses, he now had a home and a wife to keep him company. It may have been considered a strange match since he was thirty-seven and almost a confirmed bachelor, and she was just twenty-three. No doubt he was trying to be light-hearted when he wrote to his friend Karol Zagorski:

I announce solemnly (as the occasion demands) to dear Aunt Gabrynia and to you both, that I am getting married. No one can be more surprised at it than myself. However I am not frightened at all, for as you know, I am accustomed to an adventurous life and to facing terrible dangers. Moreover, I have to avow that my betrothed does not give the impression of being at all dangerous. Jessie is her name, George her surname. She is small, not at all striking-looking person (to tell the truth alas – rather plain!) who is nevertheless very dear to me. When I met her a year and a half ago she was earning her living in the City as a 'Typewriter' in an American business office of the Caligraph Company. Her father died three years ago. There are nine children in the family. The mother is a very decent women (and I do not doubt very virtuous as well) … The wedding will take place on the 24th of this month and we shall leave London immediately so as to conceal from people's eyes our happiness (or our stupidity) amidst the wilderness and beauty of the coast of Brittany where I intend to rent a small house in a fishing village.

Jessie proved an invaluable support to the highly strung author, who was always prone to self-questioning and self-doubt and likely to succumb to various illnesses, both real and at least in part a result of his acute nervousness. Conrad wrote slowly and with extraordinary care and his publisher and later his agent needed to exercise patience as well as offer financial support in the form of advances against his uncompleted stories. Jessie was calm and unflappable, a competent manager of the Conrad household, who typed and corrected his manuscripts and in due course became the mother of their two sons.

Conrad brought with him to Brittany the manuscript of *The Rescue*. He wrote to Garnett that he had completed twenty-four difficult pages and tells him that, 'I am ready to cut, slash, erase, destroy, spit, trample, jump, and wipe my feet on that MS at a word from you.'

15

The Rescue:
The Man and the Brig

He had often heard men say that Tom Lingard cared for
nothing on earth but for his brig – and in his thoughts he would
smilingly correct the statement by adding that he cared for
nothing *living* but the brig ... To him she was always
precious – like old love; always desirable – like a strange
woman; always tender – like a mother; always faithful –
like the favourite daughter of a man's heart.
Joseph Conrad, *The Rescue*, 1920

After completing *An Outcast of the Islands*, Joseph Conrad chose
to use a thinly disguised William Lingard, a well-known trader
in Singapore and the eastern islands, as the model for his next
novel, which was *The Rescue*. It is not certain that Joseph Conrad
actually met William Lingard, but in between his voyages and
during his time in Singapore, he may have heard the old mariner
spinning yarns in Emmerson's Tiffin, Billiard and Reading Rooms.
His description of the white-haired mariner talking of his Borneo

river and its people seems like a portrait drawn from real life:

> His thunderous laughter filled the verandah, rolled over
> the hotel garden, overflowed into the street, paralysing
> for a short moment the noiseless traffic of bare brown
> feet; and its loud reverberations would even startle
> the landlord's tame bird – a shameless mynah – into a
> moment's proprietary behaviour under the nearest chair.
> In the big billiard-room perspiring men in thin cotton
> singlets would stop the game, listen, cue in hand, for a
> while through the open window, then nod their moist
> faces at each other sagaciously and whisper – 'the old
> fellow is talking about his river'.

William Lingard based himself and his vessel in Singapore and from the 1840s he was active in the archipelago trade. He knew the islands, rivers and estuaries of the Dutch East Indies and the Indonesian Archipelago like the back of his hand and was always in search of new markets for his cargoes. John Dill Ross in his book *Sixty Years of Life and Adventures in the Far East* relates a story of how Lingard after finding it impossible to obtain payment of a very large sum of money for his trade goods consigned to the Sultan of Bulangan, had landed his crew and stormed the sultan's palace, after which His Highness was promptly able to find the money. And it is believed that it was this same sultan who gave William Lingard his title of 'Rajah Laut' or 'King of the Sea'.

Sailing down the coast of East Borneo, William Lingard heard that a new Malay settlement had been formed on a little-known river and that the sultanate of Gunung Tabour had recently been established there. He then surveyed the numerous channels that formed the delta at the entrance to the river and after discovering what became known as Lingard's Crossing or Oversteek van Lingard, was able to make his way forty miles upstream to the settlement. What made William Lingard different was that he had found the entrance to a river. His River!

In 1843, Christopher Nickels, later a principal of the Gutta Percha Co, attended a meeting of the Joint Committee of the Royal Society that discussed samples of gutta-percha sent from Singapore by a Dr William Montgomerie. Following that meeting Ker Rawson and Company in Singapore arranged for what became the first shipment of gutta-percha as 'an article of commerce' in 1845. The demand for gutta percha grew rapidly and it was used to produce a variety of industrial and consumer products. There was suddenly a huge demand for gutta-percha from 1850 as it could be extruded like rubber and used to cover thousands of miles of undersea cables which were being laid by *The Indian Rubber, Gutta Percha and Telegraph Works Company* to connect the world by undersea telegraph.

Many tried to follow Lingard and find that land of plenty for gutta-percha and rattan, pearl shells and birds' nests, wax and gum-dammar, but his vessel could out-sail every craft in those seas. A few of these craft came to grief on hidden sandbanks and coral reefs, others were discouraged, and for many years the green and peaceful-looking islands guarding the entrances to the Berau River kept their secret. As Conrad wrote:

His brig would usually disappear quietly during the night from the roadstead while his companions were sleeping off the effects of a midnight carouse, Lingard seeing them drunk under the table before going on board, himself unaffected by any amount of liquor.

Sailors saw his brig battling with a heavy monsoon in the South China Sea, lying becalmed in the Java Sea or suddenly gliding out from a point of land graceful and silent in the clear moonlight of the Macassar Strait. Between voyages he could be seen on the streets of Singapore, conversing in 'The Square', striding from the Occidental Bank to the Harbour Office or disappearing down a street in Chinatown. Those merchants with whom he had business could easily see that it was enough to give him his Malay title to flatter him greatly. They would drop the Captain Lingard and address him half seriously as Rajah Laut.

William Lingard's fortunes declined as steam replaced sail and it was easier to enter the shallow coastal rivers and voyage up their narrow confines into the interior, such as with a steamship like the *Vidar*. In August 1884, Lingard was forced to put his vessel *Rajah Laut* up for sale as he had lost his monopoly to the Arabs and the heyday of his Borneo trading was coming to an end. He returned to England and John Dill Ross describes a party where Lingard, in his later years, was a guest:

Lingard is an awfully decent fellow, and very generous with his dollars if anybody wants some of them, but off the quarter deck of his old barque he is a bit of a nuisance.

He'll be half-seas over before he thinks of going home tonight. Everybody concurred and everybody thought of the piles of money that Lingard made out of his gutta-percha trade.

Based on the real William Lingard, Joseph Conrad in his book *The Rescue* introduces us to his fictional and still youthful Tom Lingard. Conrad had written that James Brooke, the first White Rajah of Sarawak, was one of his boyish admirations. It is possible that he modelled this description of Tom Lingard from *The Rescue* after the heroic portrait of the young James Brooke pictured as a dashing swashbuckler with a river and jungle in the background:

He wore a grey flannel shirt, and his white trousers were held by a blue silk scarf wound tightly round his narrow waist. He had come up only for a moment, but finding the poop shaded by the main-topsail he remained on deck bareheaded. The light chestnut hair curled close about his well-shaped head, and the clipped beard glinted vividly when he passed across a narrow strip of sunlight, as if every hair in it had been a wavy and attenuated gold wire. His mouth was lost in the heavy moustache; his nose was straight, short, slightly blunted at the end; a broad band of deeper red stretched under the eyes, clung to the cheek bones. The eyes gave the face its remarkable expression. The eyebrows, darker than the hair, pencilled a straight line below the wide and unwrinkled brow much whiter than the sunburnt face. The eyes, as if glowing with the light of a hidden fire, had a red glint in their greyness that gave a scrutinising ardour to the steadiness of their gaze.

In 1835 James Brooke inherited £30,000, which he used as capital to purchase a 142-ton schooner, the *Royalist*. Setting sail for Celebes and Borneo in 1838, he arrived in Sarawak to find the settlement of Kuching in turmoil caused by an uprising against the Sultan of Brunei. Using the threat of the firepower he had brought with him, he assisted in crushing the rebellion, thereby winning the gratitude of the sultan, who in 1841 offered Brooke the governorship of Sarawak. As rajah, James Brooke pacified the natives, suppressed Dyak headhunting and with the help of the British China Squadron was highly successful in destroying the widespread piracy in the region. The rule of the White Rajah of Sarawak continued through three generations from 1842 to 1946 and it was only after the Japanese invasion and the end of the Second World War that Charles Vyner Brooke, the last White Rajah of Sarawak, ceded Sarawak to Britain.

Joseph Conrad describes the fictional Tom Lingard as a child of generations of fishermen from the coast of Devon, a Brixham trawler boy, and a youth in colliers before leaving England for Australia. Lingard cared for nothing on earth but his brig *Flash* and for his river, as described by Joseph Conrad:

The *Flash* swept slowly through the populated reach, to enter the lonely stretches of sparkling brown water bordered by the dense and silent forest, whose big trees nodded their outspread boughs gently in the faint, warm breeze – as if in sign of tender but melancholy welcome. He loved it all: the landscape of brown golds and brilliant emeralds under the dome of hot sapphire; the whispering big trees; the loquacious nipa-palms that rattled their leaves volubly in the night breeze, as if in haste to tell him all the secrets of the great forest behind them. He loved the heavy scents of blossoms and black earth, that breath of life and of death which lingered over his brig in the damp air of tepid and peaceful nights. He loved the narrow and sombre creeks, strangers to sunshine: black, smooth, tortuous–like byways of despair.

In his book *The Rescue,* Conrad describes a Singapore bar scene, probably Emmerson's, where a discussion of Tom Lingard occurred. Lingard asks his mate 'Did they speak of me' and Shaw replied:

They said many things – I take it in a jocular way, sir. They ended by being noisy too having – as I said – a great deal of cargo on board ... Yes they spoke of you. They said you were a friend of them there Malays. – and thick with some prince ... I recollect one of them saying you had a hand in some troubles with the natives in Celebes ... and that if the Dutch got hold of you it would be all over with you ... Another contradicted him and kept shouting 'There's no proof! There's no proof! ... One of them – an old chap with eye-glasses said that the existence of men like you was a diss...grace to ci-vi-li-sation.

According to Joseph Conrad, Tom Lingard was a simple man, a simple and most dangerous man. For Lingard insisted on judging the fallible and complex lives of others by his own uncomplicated moral and social standards. He was a brave man, a basically good man who, unfortunately must play God – with disastrous results. Both Kaspar Almayer and Peter Willems were his protégés and Tom Lingard was the classic example of the havoc that may be wrought by a self-righteous man who believed that his truth, was the only truth in the world.

***

In *The Rescue*, Tom Lingard's early trading activities brought him to Papua at the eastern-most end of the Indonesian Archipelago, to a place where European trade had not yet penetrated. It was here that Lingard met the young Pata Hassim, the nephew of one of the great chiefs of Wajo in South Sulawesi. Conrad describes Pata Hassim as wearing:

> A jacket of coarse blue cotton, of the kind a poor fisherman might own, and he wore it wide open on a muscular chest the colour and smoothness of bronze. From the twist of threadbare sarong wound tightly on the hips protruded outward to the left the ivory hilt, ringed with six bands of gold, of a weapon that would not have disgraced a ruler. Silver glittered about the flintlock and the hardwood stock of his gun. The red and gold handkerchief folded round his head was of costly stuff, such as is woven by

high-born women in the households of chiefs, only the gold threads were tarnished and the silk frayed in the folds ... His upright figure had a negligent elegance. But in the careless face, in the easy gestures of the whole man there was something attentive and restrained.

Lingard's brig came to anchor in the same bay and shortly afterward Pata Hassim observed a white man with four Malay crew land from a boat and stroll unarmed toward the native village. Going ashore to collect water, Lingard and his crew were involved in a misunderstanding that led to a confrontation with the locals and the death of one of their crew. They were rescued by Pata Hassim and his sister Immada, and as described by Conrad:

Lingard and the young leader of the Wajo traders met in the splendid light of noonday, and amidst the attentive silence of their followers, on the very spot where the Malay seaman had lost his life. Lingard, striding up from one side, thrust out his open palm, Hassim responded at once to the frank gesture and they exchanged their first hand-clasp over the prostrate body, as if fate had already exacted the price of a death for the most ominous of her gifts. 'I'll never forget this day,' cried Lingard.

After his rescue, Tom Lingard promised that he would soon honour Hassim and Immada by making a visit to their home country of Wajo, a Bugis regency on the south-western peninsula of Sulawesi. Joseph Conrad's knowledge of the Wajo people came from a visit there by James Brooke in 1840 who wrote a journal of his experiences which reflects his interest in the political constitutions of the Bugis kingdoms. Of particular interest is Brooke's description of the workings of Wajo's elective monarchy. The government consisted of six hereditary rajahs and six civil officers. With these six officers rested the election of a head of the state, who may be considered an elective monarch. The core rights of the free population were security of person and property, access to individual justice, freedom of movement and freedom of commercial contract.

Brooke also recorded that all the offices of state, including even that of ruler, were open to women and they actually filled the important posts of government. At the time he was there four out of the six great chiefs of Wajo were females. These women appeared in public just as the men did: they rode horses, they ruled and they received foreigners without requiring consent from their husbands. That women in South Sulawesi could hold senior positions in the state reflected a more general equality of rights between men and women. 'The Wajo women,' Brooke wrote, 'enjoy perfect liberty, and are free from all the restraints usually imposed by the Mohammedan religion'. It is evident that female equality in Wajo at this time was greater than existed in any Western system of citizenship earlier than the twentieth century, including Britain. Conrad's description of the Wajo princess Immada may give us an idea of his typical Wajo female leader:

> Her black hair hung like a mantle. Her sarong, the kilt-like garment which both sexes wear, had the national check

of grey and red, but she had not completed her attire by the belt, scarves, the loose upper wrappings, and the head-covering of a woman. A black silk jacket, like that of a man of rank, was buttoned over her bust and fitted closely to her slender waist. The edge of a stand-up collar, stiff with gold embroidery, rubbed her cheek. She had no bracelets, no anklets, and although dressed practically in man's clothes, had about her person no weapon of any sort. Her arms hung down in exceedingly tight sleeves slit a little way up from the wrist, gold-braided and with a row of small gold buttons. She walked, brown and alert, all of a piece, with short steps, the eyes lively in an impassive little face, the arched mouth closed firmly, and her whole person breathed in its rigid grace the fiery gravity of youth at the beginning of the task of life – at the beginning of beliefs and hopes.

The people of Wajo, with perhaps the keenest sense of local autonomy of any in pre-colonial Sulawesi, had become active sailors and traders in the last decades of their alliance with Macassar. Brooke thought these freedoms contributed to the success of the Wajo in commerce and their ability to establish Bugis trading settlements as far afield as Borneo, the Riau Islands and Johore on the Malay Peninsula.

On his return to Wajo from Papua, Hassim found that his Rajah was dying and a strong group had been formed to oppose the rightful successor. This was the beginning of a civil war and before Hassim could become the next rajah, he and his men were attacked by his enemies and forced to take refuge in their stockade.

When Lingard arrived off the coast of Wajo he received a message that Hassim and Immada were besieged in their stockade and were in immediate danger. Under cover of both darkness and a fierce tropical storm, Lingard sent his longboat ashore to take off Hassim and his supporters. Traditional tellers of this civil war relate in an awed tone how on a certain night:

'When there was such a thunderstorm as has been never heard of before or since' a ship, resembling the ships of white men, appeared off the coast, 'as though she had sailed down from the clouds. She moved,' he will affirm, 'with her sails bellying against the wind; in size she was like an island; the lightning played between her masts which were as high as the summits of mountains; a star burned low through the clouds above her. We knew it for a star at once because no flame of man's kindling could have endured the wind and rain of that night. It was such a night that we on the watch hardly dared look upon the sea. The heavy rain was beating down our eyelids. And when day came, the ship was nowhere to be seen, and in the stockade where the day before there were a hundred or more at our mercy, there was no one. The chief, Hassim, was gone, and the lady who was a princess in the country, and nobody knows what became of them from that day.

According to Conrad, Tom Lingard had taken them to a place which he called 'The Shore of Refuge' on the southwest coast of Borneo. The Carimata Strait, the Carimata Islands and the 'Shore of Refuge' would have been familiar to Conrad as he had frequently traversed this strait while sailing from Singapore to Macassar on the *Vidar*. 'Looking at it from seaward, the innumerable islets fringing the mainland merge into a background that presents not a single landmark to point the way through its intricate channels,' wrote Conrad. Tom Lingard was familiar with the chief man of this coast named Belarab and told Hassim and Immada that he would provide them refuge and that he would help them reconquer their country. In return for guns and money, Belarab promised his help in the reconquest of Wajo. His men were born to fight and when the time came Lingard had only to speak and a sign from Belarab would send them to what may be a vain death.

In Singapore, Lingard purchased a battered and decrepit old schooner much to the delight of its owner who bragged of the price he had got for 'that rotten old hooker'.

The *Emma* left Singapore in company with Lingard's brig and upon reaching the 'Shore of Refuge' they found their way through the narrow channels to a point far from Belarab's settlement where she was hidden in the mangroves and ran aground. All the guns and gunpowder that Lingard and his allies needed to fight their war and restore Hassim and Immada to their land were already stored on board.

***

Joseph Conrad began writing *The Rescue* after the success of *Almayer's Folly* and *The Outcast of the Islands*, but he had difficulties in completing it. Perhaps because it did not relate directly to his earlier creative phase when writing about the settlement on the Berau River. Perhaps because it was becoming a love story and he describes it himself as 'A Romance of the Shallows'. But Conrad was not good with love stories or with happy endings. He explains that he saw the action plainly enough but what he had lost was the sense of the proper expression. This weakened his confidence in its intrinsic worth and in possible interest in the story. He wrote to his agent that in nine days he could finish only one page:

> I begin to fear that I have not enough imagination – not
> enough power to make anything out of the situation. That
> I cannot invent an illuminating episode that would set in
> a clear light the persons and feelings. I am in desperation
> and I have practically given up on the book.

So, he decided to lay these difficulties aside and begin work on *The Nigger of the Narcissus* which seemed a more interesting story. Time passed and then the autobiographical story which became 'Youth' had to be put on paper before it was lost. *Heart of Darkness* was a truly compelling story, and then the saga that became *Lord Jim* was irresistible and so the manuscript of *The Rescue* lay unfinished for a long period.

16

Lord Jim

One sunny morning in the common-place surroundings
of an Eastern roadstead, I saw his form pass by – appealing
– significant – under a cloud – perfectly silent. Which is as it
should be. It was for me, with all the sympathy of which I was
capable, to seek fit words for his meaning. He was 'one of us'.
Joseph Conrad, Authors Note to *Lord Jim,* 1900

Joseph Conrad first set foot on Singapore's shores in 1883. At
the time, he was the second mate on the *Palestine*, which was
carrying coal from Newcastle to Bangkok. After the cargo self-
combusted and caused the ship to sink in March 1883, the officers
and crew were taken to Singapore the following month on the
British steamship *Sissie*. Here, the *Sissie* joined the forest of masts
anchored in the harbour while around them were hundreds of
Chinese tongkangs and Malay prows unloading goods from
trading vessels. Conrad remained in Singapore for the whole of
April and would have stayed in Sailors' Home behind St Andrew's
Cathedral. Seeking a passage back to England, he walked daily
along the Esplanade, past the white pillared façade and the

luxurious gardens of the Hotel de L'Europe, over the Cavanagh Bridge with its view of all the activity in Boat Quay, to visit the Harbour Office and then lunch with the other sailors gathered in Emmerson's Tiffin Rooms. It was during this period that he could easily have passed Austin Williams on the landing steps of Johnstone Pier, in a ship chandler's office, or on the street outside Emmerson's Tiffin Rooms.

This story of the desertion of a Singapore ship by its European officers stayed with Conrad for eighteen years and he began writing what he considered to be short story about the pilgrim ship episode. This was a new period in his life, as Conrad was now married, he had a son Borys and rent to pay. He had been living off advances from his publisher for his unpublished work; because of these circumstances, writing for pleasure had now turned into writing as a job and the creativity dried up. He would often sit at his desk in Pent Farm, looking at a blank piece of paper, and could only fill it with a few hundred words every day. He wrote to his agent, Garnett, in 1899:

> The more I write the less substance I see in my work. The scales are falling off my eyes. It is tolerably awful. And I face it, I face it but the fright is growing on me.

However, Conrad persisted with *Lord Jim* for another year, and the latter part of the story allowed him to return to the familiar territory of the Berau River and perhaps a renewed confidence. His short story eventually became a novel of many thousand words, the first of his characteristically convoluted moral tales and probably the most well-known of his Malay novels.

Born in the vicarage of Porthleven, Cornwall in 1852, Austin Williams was one of fifteen children. He came from generations of clergymen and as a boy he had learnt through his father's strict discipline the rules for proper gentlemanly conduct. While still a young man he decided on a career at sea and spent two years in a training school of the British Merchant Marine. With a gift for leadership, he had served as a ship's officer since he was twenty and had every prospect of an outstanding career. As chief officer of the *Jeddah* he oversaw the loading in Singapore of six hundred tons of sugar as well as general merchandise. The vessel then sailed from Singapore in July 1880 for Penang, where they boarded 992 Muslim pilgrims bound on a voyage to Mecca and the Holy Land. Tall and powerfully built, the twenty-eight-year-old chief officer had no premonition of the unprecedented disaster that was about to befall him, the passengers and the crew of the *Jeddah*.

Jim, the fictional version of Austin Williams, is indeed a strange kind of hero. Conrad identified him as one who had been influenced in his youth by heroic tales of adventure and the glory of Empire. Jim was one of five sons and once he declared an interest in a life at sea he was sent to a training ship for officers of the mercantile marine. He learned a little trigonometry there and gained third place in navigation. Having a steady head with an excellent physique, he was very smart aloft. His station was high in the fore-top mast and from there he looked down on others with the supreme confidence of a young man who considered himself destined to shine in the midst of dangers. However, while on the training ship he missed the chance to fulfil his heroic dreams when he failed to join a cutter to rescue a man-overboard during a storm. According to Conrad, the fictional Jim became chief mate of a fine ship, the *Patna*, without ever having been tested by those events of the sea that showed the inner worth of a man and the fibre of his being, not only to others but also to himself.

* * *

Departing Penang with every available space on the *Patna* occupied by pilgrims, it was Jim who plotted the course towards the Holy Land:

> The ship's position at last noon was marked with a small black cross, and the straight pencil-line drawn figured the course of the ship – the path of souls towards the holy place, the promise of salvation, the reward of eternal life – while the pencil with its sharp end touching the Somali coast lay round and still like a naked ship's spar floating in the pool of a sheltered dock. 'How steady she goes,' thought Jim with wonder, with something like gratitude for this high peace of sea and sky. At such times his thoughts would be full of valorous deeds: he loved these dreams and the success of his imaginary achievements. They were the best parts of life, its secret truth, and its hidden reality. They had a gorgeous virility, the charm of vagueness, they passed before him with an heroic tread, they carried his soul away with them and made it drunk with the divine philtre of an unbounded confidence in

itself. There was nothing he could not face.

Near the entrance to the Red Sea, the ship bumped into a submerged object, probably a sunken ship floating just beneath the surface. Shortly thereafter the forepart of the hold was found to be full of water and the thin collision bulkhead amidships bulged and throbbed from the pressure of water on the other side. The *Patna* was tilted head down, rear in the air, the entire ship poised for a dive to the bottom of the ocean. The chief engineer asserted to Jim that that the bulkhead would give way at any moment and the ship would go straight to the bottom.

Jim's training and all the traditions of the merchant marine had taught him that it was his responsibility to help save the passengers, even above that of saving his own life. But he knew there were nine hundred and ninety-two passengers and only seven lifeboats. Perhaps he was not afraid of death but was more afraid of the emergency. His imagination evoked for him all the horrors of the panic, the trampling rush of the desperate pilgrims, the pitiful screams, the few lifeboats overloaded and unsafe, all the appalling incidents of a disaster at sea that he could conceive. It was his responsibility to help save the passengers. His code of conduct told him he should be ready to fight a losing battle to the last, even until his own death.

The *Patna's* captain and other officers had done their own arithmetic and were busy trying to launch the lifeboats under the cover of darkness. Not for the passengers, but for themselves. They were about to violate the most basic tenet of the British Merchant Marine code. Jim shut his eyes and envisioned the pilgrims again.

Here was the chance he had been waiting for. He could be the sole European officer to remain on board and steady the ship, rescue the passengers and be a hero. Jim saw the other officers down in the lifeboat and they called up for him to join them. 'Jump! Jump!' they cried. Jim recalled the straining bulkhead, the surging sea, the nine hundred people and only seven boats. He jumped. 'I jumped ... I jumped ... I wished I could die. There was no going back. It was if I had jumped into a well – into an everlasting deep hole.'

The morning after the officers had abandoned their sinking ship they were picked up by a British steamer and taken to Aden where they reported the loss of the ship and its passengers. The next day the *Patna* arrived in Aden with all its remaining passengers still on board. According to Conrad, Jim had missed his great chance to be a hero and had humiliated himself so thoroughly that the rest of his life had to be spent in atonement.

The captain and the other ship's officers abscond before facing the Court of Inquiry in Singapore, except for Jim who decided to do the right thing. Jim insisted before the Inquiry he had preserved his honour because he believed, beyond a shadow of doubt that the ship was about to sink, before he jumped. Instead of being the hero who had stayed with the ship he was now branded as a coward who had broken an immemorial tradition of the sea. The inquiry stripped him of his officer's certificate and he remained stigmatised in the eyes of the public and his fellow seamen as a deserter from his ship in time of peril.

Conrad's alter ego, Charles Marlow, was a fictional English seaman who he used as the narrator for *Lord Jim*. Marlow attended the Singapore inquiry and wanted to understand how a seemingly stalwart English boy of good family, upbringing and training could have failed. Jim's courage in facing the inquiry and his belief that he had not broken tradition, despite all the evidence to the contrary, convinced Marlow that Jim deserved some assistance in his life and in his fight against universal condemnation. Marlow saw Jim outside the courthouse and knowing his story he was surprised at how normal he looked. Young, clean-faced, firm on his feet, who Conrad describes as promising a boy as the sun ever shone on. Marlow famously noted that Jim looked like 'one of us' – three words that have intrigued Conrad scholars ever since, suggesting to some that Jim symbolised a tragic flaw or common guilt in man – and Marlow invited Jim to dine with him at the Malabar Hotel:

A little wine opened Jim's heart and loosened his tongue. His appetite was good, too, I noticed. He seemed to have buried somewhere the opening episode of our acquaintance. It was like a thing of which there would be no more question in this world. And all the time I had before me these blue, boyish eyes looking straight into mine, this young face, these capable shoulders, the open bronzed forehead with a white line under the roots of clustering fair hair, this appearance appealing at sight to all my sympathies: this frank aspect, the artless smile, the youthful seriousness. He was of the right sort; he was one of us ... My mind floated in a sea of conjectures till the turn of the conversation enabled me, without being offensive, to remark that, upon the whole, this inquiry must have been pretty trying to him. He darted his arm across the tablecloth, and clutching my hand by the side of my plate, glared fixedly. I was startled. 'It must be awfully hard,' I stammered, confused by this display of speechless feeling. 'It is – hell,' he burst out in a muffled voice.

Based on Jim's insistence on facing the Singapore inquiry, Marlow decided to give him a letter of recommendation that would allow him to get a job in another eastern port as a water-clerk. His job was to represent his ship chandler and attempt to win the business of arriving ships before other water-clerks did the same. He would race by any means to the vessels, sweet talk the captains and steer them towards the chandler. Good water-clerks were scarce. Water-clerks with knowledge of life at sea were invaluable to their employers. Jim earned good wages, but the nature of the job meant he inevitably made contact with people who were familiar with the *Patna* affair and the role of its chief officer, and he would then suddenly throw his job and depart. Jim retreated from port to port, but the *Patna* affair inevitably followed him. Thus, over a period of years, he was known successively in Bombay, Calcutta, Rangoon, Penang, Batavia and then Bangkok. Marlow met up with Jim in Bangkok, rescuing him from a difficult situation there and took him away in his ship:

It was pitiful to see how he shrank within himself. A seaman, even if a mere passenger, takes an interest in a ship and looks at the sea-life around him with the critical enjoyment of a painter. But Jim, for the most part, skulked down below as though he had been a stowaway. For whole days we did not exchange a word; I felt extremely unwilling to give orders to my officers in his presence. Often, when alone with him on deck or in the cabin, we didn't know what to do with our eyes.

Marlow then found a job for Jim as a ship chandler in Semarang. However, he had lost some of that elasticity which had enabled him to rebound back into his position after every setback. One day, coming ashore, Marlow saw him standing on the quay waiting for his boat, which was being loaded with packages of small stores for some vessel ready to leave. After exchanging greetings, they remained silent, side by side. 'Jove!' Jim said suddenly, 'this is killing work.' Marlow retold the story of Jim's life to his friend Stein, a man who had a large inter-island business, with a number of trading posts for collecting produce in the most out-of-the-way places:

His wealth and his respectability were not exactly the reasons why I was anxious to seek his advice. I desired to confide my difficulty to him because he was one of the most trustworthy men I had ever known and considered him an eminently suitable person to receive my confidences about Jim's difficulties as well as my own. Stein diagnoses Jim's case and decides that the only possible solution for Jim is to immerse himself into a secluded segment of the world, which is his own unprofitable and practically defunct trading post called Patusan.

Jim travelled to Patusan and replaced Cornelius, a Malaccan Portuguese, who represented Stein there. Cornelius had apparently taken the liberty to appropriate to himself some of the goods of Stein's trading company and was about to be fired. A brigantine of Stein's was leaving for the westward that afternoon and could take Jim to Patusan. Except her captain was going to carry Jim only to the mouth of the river – he refused to sail further as the last time he had entered the river his vessel had been fired on from the jungle. Jim alighted at Batu Kring which is a fishing village on the coast and he was taken by canoe up the river to Patusan. Joseph Conrad's descriptions of Patusan in *Lord Jim* clearly locates it as the settlement of Sambir in *Almayer's Folly* and *An Outcast of the Islands*:

The coast of Patusan is straight and sombre, and faces a misty ocean. Red trails are seen like cataracts of rust streaming under the dark-green foliage of bushes and creepers clothing the low cliffs. Swampy plains open out at the mouth of rivers, with a view of jagged blue peaks beyond the vast forests. In the offing a chain of islands, dark, crumbling shapes, stand out in the everlasting sunlit haze like the remains of a wall breached by the sea.

Patusan is a remote district of a native-ruled state, and the chief settlement bears its name. At a point on the river about forty miles from the sea, where the first houses come into view, there can be seen rising above the level of the forest the summits of two steep hills.

Does this sound familiar?

Heeding Stein's advice and following his romantic dream, Jim buried his shame in the completely new world of Patusan. He was able to transform his failed life into a romantic and heroic success. With the help of Jewel, the mixed-race girl with whom he fell in love, he subjugated Cornelius, and then with the aid of Doramin and Dain Waris he was able to control the nominal ruler of Patusan, the Rajah Allang who could no longer exploit the settlement. No one in Singapore, in Emmerson's or in the other ports where he had worked in the past, would have recognised Jim in Patusan. By his own efforts, his own courage and goodwill, had become, so to speak, a white rajah. He built a settlement to house the liberated locals, constructed huts for them and protected their land by an earth wall with a palisade, defended by guns provided by Doramin. My own people, he called them. He had become Tuan Jim – Lord Jim – and here he was loved and trusted for his nobility and courage, something for which the seamen and the population in Singapore would never have given him credit. This was all very well and good, but Joseph Conrad would still require that Jim make the ultimate sacrifice before he could possibly redeem himself:

And that's the end. He passes away under a cloud, inscrutable at heart, forgotten, unforgiven, and excessively romantic. Not in the wildest days of his boyish visions could he have seen the alluring shape of such an extraordinary success! For it may very well be that in that short moment of his last proud and unflinching glance, he had beheld the face of that opportunity which, like an Eastern bride, had come veiled to his side.

17

Victory:
An Island Tale

Heyst hastened to slip his arm under her neck. She
felt relieved at once of an intolerable weight, and was
content to surrender to him the infinite weariness of
her tremendous achievement. Exulting, she saw herself
extended on the bed, in a black dress, and profoundly
at peace; while, stooping over her with a kindly, playful
smile, he was ready to lift her up in his firm arms and take
her into the sanctuary of his innermost heart – for ever!
The flush of rapture flooding her whole being broke out
in a smile of innocent, girlish happiness; and with that
divine radiance on her lips she breathed her last, triumphant,
seeking for his glance in the shades of death.

Victory, Joseph Conrad, 1915

The novel *Chance* published in 1913, Joseph Conrad's only story
with something like a happy ending, brought him commercial
success, especially in America. His earlier works now found

a larger reading public and for the first time in his writing life Joseph Conrad had some measure of financial security.

Conrad had the idea for another of his Malay novels and he wrote to his agent, James Pinker, with a summary of the plot:

> It has a tropical Malay setting – an unconventional man and a girl on an island under peculiar circumstances to whom enters a gang of three ruffians also of a rather unconventional sort – this intrusion producing certain psychological developments and effects. There is philosophy in it and also drama – lightly treated – meant for cultured people – a piece of literature before everything – and of course fit for general reading.

For an island, Conrad knew of Pulau Laut, located off the southeast coast of Borneo, because it was on the route the *Vidar* sailed from Singapore to Macassar and also happened to be a coaling station. Pulau Laut became the setting for his novel *Victory* and he wrote in *A Personal Record*:

> I had heard of him [Almayer] in a place called Pulau Laut from a half-caste gentleman there, who described himself as the manager of a coal-mine; which sounded civilised and progressive till you heard that the mine could not be worked at present because it was haunted by some particularly atrocious ghosts.

***

221

Conrad wrote it was his unconventional man, named Axel Heyst, who having reached the island, observed the outcrops of coal and wrote of this in letters to his friends in Europe.

Accordingly, a prospectus was issued for investors in The Tropical Belt Coal Company of London and Amsterdam, which was based on the island Conrad called Samburan. The prospectus showed a circle of some eight hundred miles to indicate how the island was centrally located and connected to the ports of Manila, Saigon, Singapore and Batavia. Engineers came out and coolies were brought in to construct the settlement, a shaft was driven into the hillside and actually recovered some coal. But not enough coal for the company to be profitable and it went into liquidation. As Conrad wrote in the first chapter:

> The world of finance then is a mysterious world in which as incredible as the fact may appear, evaporation precedes liquidation. First the capital evaporates and then the company goes into liquidation. These are very unnatural physics.

Heyst, styled in the prospectus as 'manager in the tropics', remained at his post on Samburan, even as the abandoned settlement on the island was slowly invaded by the jungle. Axel Heyst is another of Conrad's flawed protagonists. Heyst said that his father had written a lot of books and was a philosopher who had imbued him, in his youth, with a deep mistrust of life. The father had advised his son, at his most impressionable age, that to avoid the tragedies of life he should avoid participating in human action – 'Look on and make no sound' were the last words of a man who had tried to change the world. Accordingly, Heyst had lived as a restless wanderer, who seem to prefer solitude and shun company.

Konrad's father Apollo was consumed by two passions: his love of literature and a fierce desire to liberate his country from Russian domination. He moved to Warsaw in 1861 where he became involved in publishing a political pamphlet, formed the underground City Committee and played a prominent role in the revolutionary activities of the period. For these activities, Apollo and his wife Ewe were arrested, convicted of seditious activities and sentenced to exile in an internment camp at Volgoda in northern Russia, together with their young son. Conrad must have been deeply affected by the heroic nature of his parents' protest, for he had seen their idealism result only in the miseries of exile and their deaths. It is possible that the advice given by the father to Heyst, was the same advice given to an eleven-year-old Joseph Conrad when his own father was dying.

After a year or more of isolation on Samburan, Axel Heyst travelled to Surabaya and happened to stay in the Schomberg Hotel. It is here that a young woman called Lena who played violin in an orchestra managed by the cruel Zangiacomo couple captured his attention:

She had captured Heyst's awakened faculty of observation; he had the sensation of a new experience. That was because his faculty of observation had never before been captured by any feminine creature in that marked and exclusive fashion.

Heyst observed how she was badly treated and tried to comfort her. She told him of herself and of her miserable past in a voice that he found charming. The next day she managed to give him a glance of tenderness that touched his heart and he began to plan her rescue from the Zangiacomo couple.

It was a shock to him, on coming out of his brown study, to find the girl so near to him, as if one waking suddenly should see the figure of his dreams turned into flesh and blood. She did not raise her shapely head, but her glance was no dream thing. It was real, the most real impression of his detached existence – so far.

Heyst abducted Lena and carried her off to the lonely island of Samburan, where she is changed from a young girl into a mature woman, genuinely in love with Heyst. As a result of the natural instincts of a loving woman, her weakness changed to strength and determination. The victory of the title is that at the story's dramatic climax, she succeeded at the cost of her own life in freeing Heyst from his father's paralysing influence and forcing him to acknowledge his love for her.

18

The Rescue:
Claim of Life
and Toll of Death

Of the three long novels of mine which suffered an
interruption, *The Rescue* was the one that had to wait the
longest for the good pleasure of the Fates. I am betraying no
secret when I state here that it had to wait for precisely twenty
years. I laid it aside at the end of the summer of 1898 and it was
about the end of the summer of 1918 that I took it up again
with the firm determination to see the end of it and helped by
a sudden feeling that I might be equal to the task.
Joseph Conrad, Introduction to *The Rescue, 1920*

The manuscript of *The Rescue* lay unfinished for twenty years.
But Conrad was not going to give up on his story. Even after so
many years the material for the book still lay there and slowly
the urge to complete the manuscript returned. He may have
also wondered, now in the twilight of his writing career, how
many books he left in him. He was sixty-one years old, crippled

by several physical ailments, and aware that his powers were diminishing. In his introduction to *The Rescue*, he explained his return to this novel after such a long absence:

> This does not mean that I turned to it with elation. I was well aware and perhaps even too much aware of the dangers of such an adventure ... As I moved slowly towards the abandoned body of the tale it loomed up big amongst the glittering shallows of the coast, lonely but not forbidding. There was nothing about it of a grim derelict. It had an air of expectant life. One after another I made out the familiar faces watching my approach with faint smiles of amused recognition. They had known well enough that I was bound to come back to them. But their eyes met mine seriously, as was only to be expected since I, myself felt very serious as I stood amongst them again after years of absence. At once, without waiting words, we went to work together on our renewed life; and every moment I felt more strongly that 'They Who had Waited' bore no grudge to the man who, however widely he may have wandered at times, had played truant only once in his life.

Twenty years after his first attempt at *The Rescue*, he was now a much more experienced writer. He began working again on *The Rescue* in 1918 and it took another two years for him to work through its difficulties or his difficulties. The main difficulty with the story for Conrad and many of his readers was that Lingard's infatuation with Mrs Travers required that he sacrifice his Malay friends, Hassim and Immada, to save Mrs Travers and the other Europeans, who some would think should have been left to fend for themselves.

* * *

Sailing from Singapore, it was now time for Tom Lingard to act on his promise to help Hassan and Immada reconquer their country. He reached the Carimata Strait and the 'Shore of Refuge' where the *Emma,* and Hassan and Immanda, were hidden. However, he and his brig *Lightning* were becalmed, there was no wind, and for hours they lay a few miles to the west of Carimata barely changing position.

Just before dusk one of the Malay crew sighted a vessel in the distance, but thought nothing of it until in the dead of night a boat with five men hailed their ship. Their leader, Carter, was allowed to come aboard and explained that they were from the schooner *Hermit* en route from Manila to Batavia, that their ship was stuck hard and fast on a mudbank about sixty miles away, and that they were one of two boats that have been sent off with a letter from the owner asking for assistance:

Lingard took the letter out of an open envelope, addressed to the commander of any British ship in the Java Sea. The paper was thick, had an embossed heading: 'Schooner-yacht *Hermit*' and was dated four days before. The message said that on a hazy night the yacht had gone ashore upon some outlying shoals off the coast of Borneo. The land was low. The opinion of the sailing-master was that the vessel had gone ashore at the top of high water, spring tides. The coast was completely deserted to all appearance. During the four days they had been stranded there they had sighted in the distance two small native vessels, which did not approach. The owner concluded by asking any commander of a homeward-bound ship to report the yacht's position in Anjer on his way through Sunda Straits – or to any British or Dutch man-of-war he might meet. The letter ended by anticipatory thanks, the offer to pay any expenses in connection with the sending of messages from Anjer, and the usual polite expressions.

Lingard quickly realised that the presence of a British or Dutch gunboat would completely upset his well-laid plans and decided that he should attempt to rescue the schooner himself as soon as possible. With the *Hermit's* boat in tow, the *Lightning* made its way towards the location of the schooner. Lingard's plan was to take all the people off the schooner onto his brig for a week while he and his crew removed every scrap of ballast and extra weight, until the *Hermit* could then be floated off on the next high tide and he could say goodbye to them forever.

Mr Travers, the owner of the *Hermit* was not a happy man. Mr Travers displayed money, and was dressed like a yachtsman in white pants and blue blazer, full of his own self-importance. Lingard struggled to convince Travers to abandon his yacht while he stripped it down, as Travers judged Lingard to be only interested in getting a lot of salvage money out of a stranded vessel:

'I don't see my way to utilise your services,' he says, with
cold finality. 'Perhaps it's just as well,' says Lingard,
'because I did not offer my services. I've offered to take
you on board my brig for a few days, as your only chance
of safety. And you asked me what were my motives. My
motives! If you don't see them they are not for you to
know.'

These men, who two hours before had never seen each other,
stood face-to-face as if they had been life-long enemies. This
was the difference between the passive, sterile and mannered
world of the *Hermit* and the active world of the *Lightning*. Mrs
Travers was in a loveless marriage and described her husband as
'enthusiastically devoted to the nursing of his own career'. In his
short time on board the schooner Lingard became convinced that
it was Mrs Travers that would listen to him. He was a man of
action and of all the women he knew, she alone seemed to be
made for action. Conrad's description of Edith Travers shows that
Lingard is stricken by her and sees her as his female counterpart:

She was tall, supple, moving freely. Her complexion was
so dazzling in the shade that it seemed to throw out a
halo round her head. Upon a smooth and wide brow an
abundance of pale fair hair, fine as silk, undulating like the
sea, heavy like a helmet, descended low without a trace
of gloss, without a gleam in its coils, as though it had

never been touched by a ray of light; and a throat white, smooth, palpitating with life, a round neck modelled with strength and delicacy, supported gloriously that radiant face and that pale mass of hair unkissed by sunshine.

***

This set up the moral dilemma and the problems that Lingard would have to face. Lingard had to resolve a divided loyalty between Hassim and Immada and the stranded white sailors. Did his priorities lie with his Malay friends or with Mr Travers and Mrs Travers? How long before the other boat with Travers' message reached the Dutch authorities and a gunboat was despatched? What about his obvious infatuation with Edith Travers?

Conrad was finally successful in completing the book. It was the last of his Malay novels and took him back to the eastern seas, to the islands of the archipelago, to his days on the trading ship *Vidar* and his first novels. In a letter to his publisher, Conrad clearly outlines the sense of the story:

The human interest of the tale is in the contact of Lingard the simple, masterful, imaginative adventurer with a type of civilised woman – a complex type. He is a man tenacious of purpose, enthusiastic in undertaking, faithful in friendship. He jeopardises the success of his plans first to assure her safety and then absolutely sacrifices his Malay friends to what he believes is the necessary condition of her happiness. He is throughout mistrusted by the whites whom he wishes to save and he is unwillingly forced into a contest with his Malay friends. Then when the rescue, for which he has sacrificed all the interests in his life, is accomplished, he has to face his reward – an inevitable separation. This episode of his life lifts him out of himself; I want to convey in the action of the story the stress and exaltation of the man under the influence of a sentiment which he hardly understands and yet which is real enough to make him go on reckless of the consequences.

For their last moments together, Conrad had Tom Lingard and Mrs Travers alone on a sandbank before dawn and he wrote:

Mrs Travers let fall her arm and began to retrace her steps, unsupported and alone. Lingard followed her on the edge of the sand uncovered by the ebbing tide. A belt of orange light appeared in the cold sky above the black forest of the Shore of Refuge and faded quickly to gold that melted soon into a blinding and colourless glare. It was not till after she had passed Jaffir's grave that Mrs Travers stole a backward glance and discovered that she was alone. Lingard had left her to herself. She saw him sitting near the mound of sand, his back bowed, his hands clasping his knees, as if he had obeyed the invincible call of his great visions haunting the grave of the faithful messenger. Shading her eyes with her hand Mrs Travers watched the immobility of that man of infinite illusions. He never moved, he never raised his head. It was all over. He was done with her. She waited a little longer and then went slowly on her way.

The reviews of *The Rescue* and especially of the love interest between Lingard and Mrs Travers were mixed. Conrad responded by saying that if only at the end of the story he had Mrs Travers hang her arms around Lingard's neck for five minutes before they separated, then everyone would have been happy.

Epilogue

Joseph Conrad was now sixty-one years old, suffering from several physical ailments and afraid that his powers were diminishing. He was proud of *The Rescue*, it had occupied his thoughts for twenty-three years and to finish it after all this time was for himself a form of rescue for it confirmed that his literary powers had not diminished. He was to publish his next and last book *The Rover* in 1923. Due to a long illness, the image of him at this time, was of a man aged and worn producing his work with meticulous care in a secluded country home in Kent. He broke his long-standing habit of wanting to talk far into the night with friends who visited him for a few days or a few hours, covering a wide range of subjects and giving proof of an amazing breadth of knowledge and a constant lack of affectation. As described by his friend and biographer Gerard Jean-Aubrey, Conrad would sometimes be:

> Huddled into himself, giving an observer the impression he was crushed by the weight of his memories, he sometimes remained for long moments in silence. In the course of a conversation, by means of a name, of a landscape recalled, one saw him sink into a profound meditation, opaque, impenetrable, like a ship plunged out

of sight, and none of us at such moments could break this silence, not only out of respect for the reverie of this great mind, but more because of a sort of physical impossibility which literally held you chained, until the moment when he emerged again like a rock the receding wave uncovers. At times these silences had for us something so profound, so anguishing, that one wished to break them at any price. Yet one could not bring oneself to do it.

At the beginning of August 1824 Conrad went to look over a new rental house but was forced to turn back as he felt ill. A few days later, on 3 August, at the age of sixty-six, Conrad died of a heart attack. Young enough for there to have been general expectation of perhaps a decade of writing still before him, it would be an understatement to say that his death was a shock. It was an enormous blow. Even those who did not know him felt it personally. His appeal had been to the heart as well as to intelligence and tribute was universal.

Conrad is buried in a cemetery at Canterbury, Kent, in the countryside he had long loved. He once spoke of the best friend of his work as being 'the cool green light on the fields'. Restless as he was by nature, he had been held by Kent for fifteen years: first Aldington, then Orlestone, and for the last five years Bishopsboume. He is now there forever. The granite block on his grave bears no cross and is inscribed with his anglicized Polish name, Joseph Teador Conrad Korzeniowski, born December 3rd 1857 and died August 3rd 1924. The inscription is a quotation from Edmund Spenser's *Faerie Queene* which Conrad had used on the title page of his last published novel, *The Rover*:

Sleep after Toyle, Port after Stormie Seas,
Ease after Warre, Death after Life Does Greatly Please.

Conrad's greatness lies in the ability in his writing to create an absolutely convincing illusion of reality. The place he now occupies in letters is as the English critic Walter Allen wrote: 'Conrad's best work represents a body of achievement unequalled in English fiction this century by any writer except Henry James.' Moreover, Henry James wrote in a letter to Conrad: 'No one has known – for intellectual use – the things you know, and you have, as the artist of the whole matter, an authority that no one has approached.'

For Joseph Conrad his greatest honour was to have his novels regarded as English classics in his own lifetime and despite the fact English was not his native language.

Joseph Conrad's life journey was a profound one, not just through the physical realms of Asia's nineteenth-century landscapes but through the emotional and intellectual voyages that shaped his literary genius. This book has been an attempt not just to trace the routes of a young mariner who would become one of the English language's most celebrated authors but to understand the essence of the experiences that fuelled his early Malay works.

In retracing Conrad's steps, we have seen how his encounters with the people and cultures of Southeast Asia informed his worldview and enriched his storytelling. Through the bustling port of Singapore to the secluded reaches of an East Borneo river, Conrad's adventures in the East Indies served as the crucible for his narrative mastery. These landscapes, vibrant with diversity and complexity, did not merely provide a backdrop for his stories but became integral characters themselves, shaping the lives and destinies of his fictional creations.

Bibliography

Allen, Jerry. *The Thunder and the Sunshine*. New York: Putnam and Sons, 1958

Allen, Jerry. *The Sea Years of Joseph Conrad*. London: Methuen and Company, 1967

Batchelor, John. *The Life of Joseph Conrad*. London: Blackwell Publishers, 1994

Beekman, Daniel. *A Voyage to the Island of Borneo*. London: Warner and Batley, 1718

Bock, Carl. *The Head-Hunters of Borneo*. Singapore: Oxford University Press, 1985

Burnet, Ian. *East Indies*. Sydney: Rosenberg Publishing, 2013

Burnet, Ian. *Archipelago*. Sydney: Rosenberg Publishing, 2015

Conrad, Joseph. *Almayer's Folly*. Oxford: Oxford University Press, 1992

Conrad, Joseph. *Victory*. Oxford: Oxford University Press, 1986

Conrad, Joseph. *An Outcast of the Islands*. Oxford: Oxford University Press, 1992

Conrad, Joseph. *The Mirror of the Sea*. Oxford: Oxford University Press, 1988

Conrad, Joseph. *A Personal Record*. Oxford: Oxford University Press, 1988

Conrad, Joseph. *Lord Jim*. Oxford: Oxford University Press, 1983

Conrad, Joseph. *The Shadow-Line*. London: J.M. Dent, 1920

Conrad, Joseph. *The End of the Tether*. London: William Blackwood, 1902

Conrad, Joseph. *The Rescue*. London: J.M. Dent, 1920

Conrad, Joseph. 'Youth'. New York: Dutton, 1920

Conrad, Joseph. *Typhoon*. London: Heinemann, 1921

Conrad, Joseph. *A Set of Six*. London: Methuen, 1920

Conrad, Joseph. 'Notes on Life and Letters'. London: J.M. Dent, 1921

Conrad, Joseph. *Twixt Land and Sea*. London: J.M. Dent, 1947

Conrad, Joseph. Within the Tides. London: J.M. Dent, 1915

Jasanoff, Maya. *The Dawn Watch*. New York: Penguin Press, 2017

Jean-Aubrey, Gerard. *The Sea Dreamer*. London: Archon Books, 1967

Karl, Frederick. *Joseph Conrad: The Three Lives*. London: Faber and Faber, 1979

Osbourn, Andreas. *A Study in Non-Conformity*. New York: Philosophical Library, 1959

Rutter, Owen. *The Pirate Wind*. Singapore: Oxford University Press, 1986

Sherry, Norman. *Conrad's Western World*. London: Cambridge University Press, 1971

Sherry, Norman. *Conrad's Eastern World*. London: Cambridge University Press, 1966

Stape, John. *The Several Lives of Joseph Conrad*. New York: Pantheon Books, 2007

Villiers, Peter. *Joseph Conrad, Master Mariner*. New York: Sheridan House, 2006

Watt, Ian. *Conrad in the Nineteenth Century*. London: Chatto and Windus, 1980

Young, Gavin. *In Search of Conrad*. London: Penguin, 1991